ICE CREAM MADE EASY

By the same author

Fresh Bread in the Morning from your Bread Machine
Slow Cooking: Best New Recipes
The Blender Book
Steaming!
Super Soups & Sauces
The Combination Microwave Book
Microwave Cooking Times at a Glance!

ICE CREAM MADE EASY

HOMEMADE RECIPES FOR ICE CREAM MACHINES

Annette Yates

Constable & Robinson Ltd
3 The Lanchesters
162 Fulham Palace Road
London W6 9ER
www.constablerobinson.com

Originally published in the UK 2004 under the title *Ice 'n' Easy*

This edition published by Right Way,
an imprint of Constable & Robinson, 2009

A copy of the British Library Cataloguing in Publication Data is available from the British Library

ISBN: 978-0-7160-2226-8

Printed and bound in the EU

CONTENTS

DEDICATION

This book is for my daughters Emma and Lindsay – avid fans of my art.

ACKNOWLEDGEMENTS

My thanks go to Gaggia, Magimix and Philips for their generosity in supplying ice cream machines with which to test the recipes in this book.

1

FROZEN ASSETS

Make no mistake, I adore making ices in my ice cream machine. It's the spontaneity, the sheer indulgence and the satisfaction of creating a luscious, frozen concoction out of a few well-chosen ingredients that makes me happy. It means I can make any flavour that takes my fancy and the choice of ingredients is up to me. Unlike many commercial products, *my* ices contain no thickeners, emulsifiers, artificial flavourings and colouring, preservatives or stabilisers.

Admittedly, making my own ice cream is not cheap – using the best fresh ingredients often costs more than a tub of ready-made. Nonetheless, in all the years I have used an ice cream machine, the only time I have been tempted to buy a carton is to check the flavour before making a similar (and usually better) one myself.

Frosty treats like creamy ice cream, light-and-airy frozen yogurts, silky sorbets, frozen desserts and slushy drinks seem to appeal to most of us, no matter what our age. In this book there is something to suit every occasion.

The recipes in *Ice Cream Made Easy* are all nice and easy! There are no difficult methods involved – just simple ingredients that require minimal preparation before being freeze-churned in the ice cream machine. In fact, they are likely to be the easiest ices you have ever made.

2

ICE CREAM MACHINES

There is no doubt that ice cream made in a machine is smoother, creamier and lighter than one made by hand. In a machine, the same ingredients will make a larger quantity of ice cream too.

An ice cream machine works by gradually freezing the ice cream mixture while simultaneously churning it to a creamy concoction. It's this churning process that makes the finished ice smooth, light and airy – by keeping the mixture moving, it prevents the formation of large ice crystals and beats in air.

When choosing an ice cream machine, always look at the manufacturer's booklet before buying. Are the instructions clear? Is there a good selection of recipes? Is the machine easy to use and clean?

A fully automatic ice cream machine with a built-in freezer unit is not cheap. However, if you love making a quick batch of ice cream at a moment's notice, just when the fancy takes you, and you have plenty of space on your kitchen worktop, you will probably consider it worth the investment. In my experience this type of machine makes ice cream with the silkiest consistency and never fails to draw envious comments from visiting friends.

In all models, the freezer unit (or compressor) is cleverly built in to the neat body of the machine.

In some models the motor is housed in the body of the machine and the paddle is powered from the base of the bowl to make the churning process smooth, secure and fairly quiet (see Fig. 1). In others the motor unit and paddle are attached to the lid (as in Fig. 2 on page 10), which can make them slightly fiddlier to use and to clean.

To make ice cream, you simply switch on the freezer unit and wait a few minutes until the correct temperature is reached. Then switch on the paddle and, while it is turning, add the ingredients and leave the rest to the machine. While

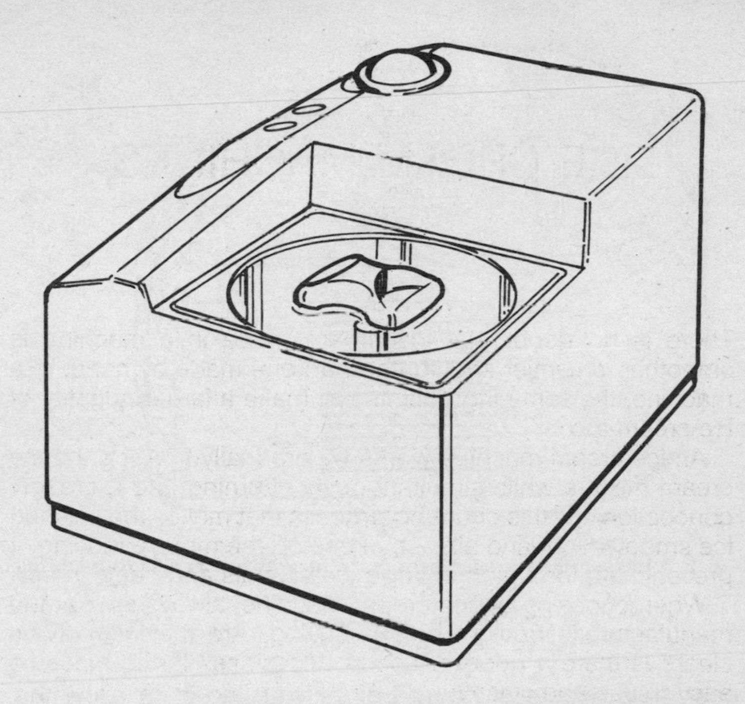

Fig. 1. A fully automatic ice cream machine with the paddle in the base.

you get on with other things, the machine automatically gets on with freezing and churning so that, just about 20 minutes later, your ice cream will be ready.

The machine usually comes with a removable bowl that sits inside the main, fixed bowl. The chief advantage is its ease of removal and cleaning, though it will of course be smaller than the main bowl (and will therefore make slightly less ice cream). To use it, you will need to pour a conductive material such as alcohol or salt solution between the two bowls – the manufacturer's instructions will give full details.

It's worth mentioning that all these machines are fairly bulky and heavy. Also, they do not take well to being moved around (the working balance of the freezing unit can be disturbed) so you will need to find an area of kitchen worktop that you can devote exclusively to your ice cream machine. On the occasions when you do need to move it, do so with care and make sure the machine is kept upright. If you really must keep it in a cupboard, be sure to put it in its working

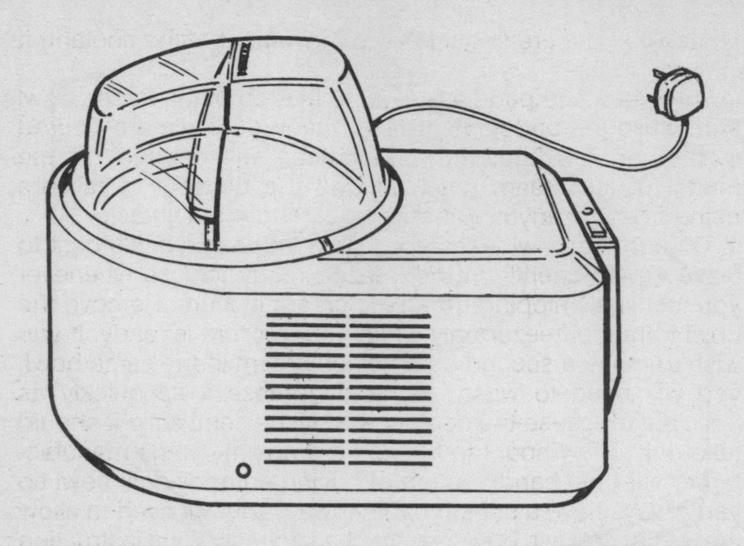

Fig. 2. A fully automatic ice cream machine with the paddle fitted in the lid.

position a couple of hours before you use it (to allow the coolant inside it to settle).

One final note! If, like me, you are likely to want to make several batches of ice cream (with different flavours perhaps) one after the other, you will probably need a machine with a paddle that is powered from the base of the bowl. These models don't usually require a rest period between uses, so you can simply give the bowl a quick wipe out before adding the next batch of ingredients.

An ice cream machine with a detachable bowl (see Fig. 3 opposite) is easily more affordable than a fully automatic model and is capable of making small quantities of lovely ice cream. Some are more efficient than others at preventing large ice crystals forming, which means that the texture of the ice cream can differ slightly from model to model, and they tend to be more noisy than the automatic machines.

The detachable bowl contains a coolant that is sealed in its walls (shake the bowl and you will hear, and feel, it sloshing around). Before using, the bowl needs to be pre-frozen in the freezer, usually for 12–24 hours depending on the model. During freezing, it must be placed upright – so that the coolant is evenly distributed. Once it is completely frozen (shake it and there should be no movement of the coolant) it is ready to use.

The motorised paddle is fixed to the top of the frozen bowl and, while the paddle is turning, the ingredients are poured in through the chute. Churning time will depend on the model of ice cream machine and the quantity of mixture being frozen – anything between 20 and 40 minutes.

Though the bowl takes up quite a lot of space, it's best to leave it permanently in the freezer, ready for use whenever you feel like whipping up an ice cream mixture. Remove the bowl from the freezer only when your mixture is ready. If you wish to make a second batch of ice cream in the same bowl, you will need to wash, dry and refreeze it as quickly as possible (because the coolant will still be semi-solid it should take only a few hours to freeze hard again). Some manufacturers offer the handy option of buying an additional bowl so you always have a standby. Either way, you will need to allow the motor to rest between batches (check your instruction book for details).

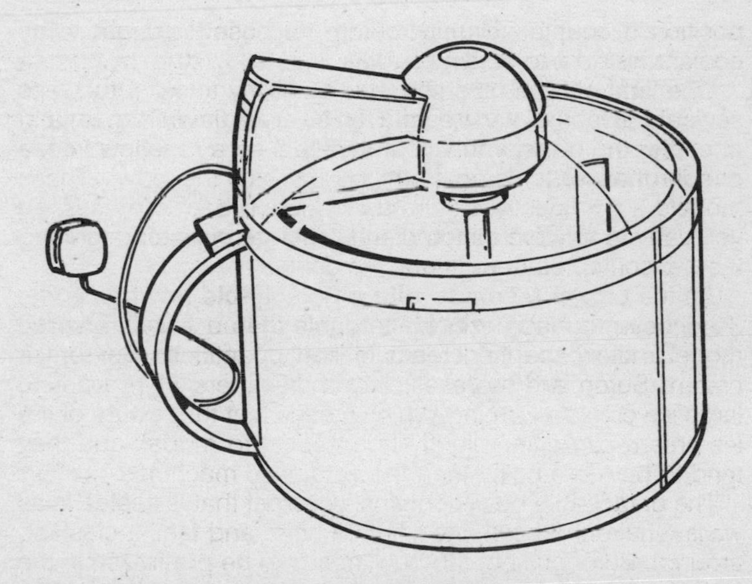

Fig. 3. An ice cream machine with a detachable bowl.

Step-by-step Method

1. Prepare the ingredients and chill them well.

2. Prepare or assemble the ice cream machine following the manufacturer's instructions.

3. Switch on the paddle.

4. With the paddle turning, pour the chilled mixture through the feed tube into the machine. (If the paddle is not turning, the mixture will freeze to the side of the bowl, after which you won't be able to make the paddle turn.)

5. Leave the mixture to churn and freeze for the required time or until the desired consistency is reached.

6. As soon as the paddle struggles to turn, stops or turns in the opposite direction, switch the machine off. At this stage the ice cream will be soft enough to spoon.

7. To firm it up slightly, ready for eating straight away, simply remove the paddle and allow the mixture to stand in the machine for 10–15 minutes. Otherwise, remove the paddle and (with a non-metal spatula or spoon) transfer the ice cream to a large, shallow freezer container.

8. Stir in any extra ingredients, such as nuts, chocolate or biscuits. Seal and label the container.

9. Put into the freezer for a couple of hours until required, to allow the ice cream to firm up and its flavours to develop and settle.

3

NO ICE CREAM MACHINE?

If you don't have an ice cream machine, you can still make ice cream, sorbet and, in particular, granita (which is meant to be crunchy with large ice crystals). Of course the process will take longer, it will require some effort on your part and the ice cream is unlikely to be as smooth and light as that made by machine.

Once the ingredients are combined, the mixture is put into the freezer. You will need to stir it often, to break up the ice crystals and beat in air so the texture of the ice becomes as smooth as possible. It's worth remembering that ice creams made with custard are naturally smooth and require less stirring than lighter mixtures.

About an hour before you intend to make ice cream, remember to turn the freezer on to 'fast freeze' or to the coldest setting (the quicker the mixture freezes, the better its texture will be). Using a shallow plastic container helps the ice cream to freeze faster too, particularly if its base and sides are in contact with the walls of the freezer.

Step-by-step Method

1. Chill the mixture well before putting it into the freezer.

2. Cover and freeze for about 1½–2 hours, stirring every 30 minutes, scraping the ice crystals that form around the edges to the centre of the container. It's a good idea to set a timer to remind you when it's time to take the mixture out of the freezer and stir it.

3. Once the mixture is part-frozen and mushy, tip it into a chilled bowl and, using a fork, mash the icy mixture. Alternatively, use an electric hand mixer to whisk it until smooth or buzz it quickly in a food processor. Whichever method you use, you will need to be quick to prevent the ice melting.

4. Return the mixture to its container, cover and return it to the freezer.

5. Each hour, repeat the mashing process in step 3 until the ice cream is thick and creamy.

6. Stir in any extra ingredients, such as nuts, chocolate or biscuits.

7. Return the mixture to its container, cover and freeze until required.

4

THE MAIN INGREDIENTS

Remember: the quality of the ice cream or sorbet will depend on the ingredients you use. The best and freshest produce will reward you with the finest ices.

Milk
Whole milk gives the smoothest, creamiest result, whether you are making ice cream, sorbet or drinks. Semi-skimmed milk and skimmed milk are particularly good for iced drinks. Keep all milk chilled until you need to use it.

Cream
The higher the fat content of the cream, the richer and creamier the ice cream. Use double cream for silky smooth ice cream and single or whipping for a lighter texture (there is no need to whip it before adding it to the ice cream maker). If you want to be really indulgent, try clotted cream (see Strawberries and Clotted Cream on page 39). Like milk, cream should always be used chilled.

Yogurt
Standard pasteurised yogurts, plain or flavoured, are best for making ice cream. I usually avoid using the live varieties unless I am making a slushy drink that is to be consumed immediately. Keep them all chilled before use.

Fromage Frais, Ricotta and Mascarpone
I have used each of these soft cheeses to make ice cream. Fromage frais and ricotta impart a light, slightly grainy texture, while mascarpone produces a rich and velvety texture. Use them straight from the refrigerator.

Condensed Milk
Used in place of custard, condensed milk makes a smooth and creamy ice cream. It's particularly good in fruit-based mixtures.

Evaporated Milk
Evaporated milk is also a good replacement for cream, though it is best used with ingredients that have good strong flavours.

Soya Milk and Cream
Use these in place of cream and milk to make mouth-watering dairy-free ices. Try some of the recipes on pages 79 to 83. Chill them until you need to use them.

Tofu
Together with soya milk and cream, tofu or soya bean curd is really useful for making non-dairy ices. It has a bland taste that readily absorbs flavours. Silken tofu gives the smoothest finish. Use it straight from the refrigerator.

Eggs
Adding egg yolks to an ice cream mixture improves its texture and gives it a rich and smooth taste.

Egg whites are useful for adding to sorbets. Because they hold air when lightly whisked, the finished sorbet will be light and fluffy.

Always make sure eggs are as fresh as possible. Cracked ones should not be used for fear of introducing bacteria to the ice cream or sorbet mixture. Keep them chilled until you need to use them.

Please also see the note on eggs on page 25.

Sugar
I usually use caster sugar because it dissolves readily and is very sweet. Sugars such as soft brown, muscovado and demerara can vary in their sweetness, so if you use these, remember to taste the mixture (and adjust it if necessary) before putting it into the ice cream machine. Dark sugars also add a richness of flavour that may (or may not) be appropriate in your mixture.

There are a couple of points worth remembering about sweetness. Firstly, freezing reduces the sensation of sweetness and flavour, so you will need to make the mixture slightly over-sweet and over-flavoured. Secondly, too much sugar will prevent the mixture from freezing properly; while too little will cause it to freeze too hard (and the flavour won't be so good).

A jar of glucose syrup is a handy standby. Add a small amount to an ice cream if you want to prevent it from freezing too hard (as in Mango Ice Cream on page 37).

Honey, Golden Syrup and Maple Syrup

I tend to add these for their flavour rather than for their sweetness. Because of their liquid consistency, adding them as the main sweetening ingredient is likely to spoil the flavour and texture of the ice cream.

Fruit

Almost any fruit can be put into ice cream or sorbet. For the best flavour use fresh fruits when they are in season and always make sure they are ripe and in the peak of condition. Add them raw for a truly fresh flavour (as in Strawberry Pavlova Ripple on page 35) or cooked for an intense flavour that will last longer in the freezer (as in Bramble Ice Cream on page 34).

When using dried fruit, choose the best, softest and plumpest fruit with a good flavour – apricots, blueberries, cranberries and raisins are particularly good.

Cans, jars and cartons of fruit and fruit compote can be made into delicious ice creams and sorbets too.

Nuts

Nuts add their flavour and texture to the simplest mixture (like Apricot and Almond Ice on page 41). Try using walnuts, pecans, almonds, hazelnuts or pistachios. Almonds and hazelnuts give a better flavour if they are lightly toasted first.

Like all the other ingredients, nuts should be used as fresh as possible – taste them before adding to the ice cream mixture – a few stale nuts can taint the entire mix with their off taste.

Coconut lovers will enjoy adding desiccated coconut for its texture and coconut cream or coconut milk for their distinctive, creamy flavour (see Coconut and Lime Ice Cream on page 52).

Chocolate

The type of chocolate I use in ice cream depends on the occasion and the mood I am in. There are times when only the best dark chocolate, with 50–70 per cent cocoa solids, will do. Then there are other times when a bar of milk chocolate confectionary seems the perfect choice for melting or chopping into ice cream – try dairy milk, fruit and nut, caramel, mint crisp, or Turkish bars, and whole chocolate buttons are good stirred in at the last moment.

Coffee

Always use a good quality coffee and add it in small amounts until the flavour is just right. I like to use strong filter coffee or a superior instant espresso.

Vanilla and Other Flavourings

I always use vanilla extract rather than vanilla essence or flavouring. The best flavour though will come from the freshly-scraped-out seeds of a vanilla pod (as in Vanilla Ice Cream with Fresh Custard on page 28). Use the seeds in ice cream and put the empty pods in a jar of golden caster sugar where it will gently flavour it for all sorts of uses.

Gelatine

A little gelatine added to a sorbet or ice cream helps to stabilise the mixture and to give it a smooth texture. By helping to retain air, it also helps to prevent sorbet from freezing too hard.

Alcohol

A spoonful of brandy, rum, whisky or liqueur will add its unique flavour to an ice cream or sorbet, turning it into something really special.

Alcohol slows down the freezing process so that you will have a softer ice that is easy to scoop. Take care not to add too much though, or it will slow down the freezing process too drastically!

5

COOL TIPS FOR MAKING, STORING AND SERVING ICES

- Use the best ingredients so that your ice cream machine will churn out the finest, most luscious of ices.

- All types of ice cream and sorbet taste best when they are still fresh, so don't be tempted to make them too far ahead of time. I usually like to make mine in the morning ready for eating later on the same day. After all, what's the point of freezing them for days or weeks when it's no hassle to make a fresh batch any time you need it.

- Chilling ingredients in your refrigerator before pouring into the machine will help to reduce the freezing and churning time.

- Use the correct quantities for your particular machine – check with your instruction book for the recommended minimum and maximum. If you overfill the bowl, the ice cream or sorbet may not freeze correctly and it will probably spill out as it bulks up and its volume increases. If the bowl is under-filled, the mixture is likely to freeze too soon without sufficient churning. Filling the bowl one-half to two-thirds full is generally a good guide.

- Mixtures containing alcohol or a high sugar content generally take longer to freeze.

- Hygiene is really important when making and storing ice cream. To prevent the development of bacteria, make sure that the ice cream machine and all containers and utensils are spotlessly clean, especially the parts that come into contact with the mixture.

To Ripple Ice Cream
Some of my favourite ices are those with a fruit syrup or caramel sauce ripple running through them. Don't try to add the sauce to the ice cream machine, even for the final few turns of the paddle – it will simply blend in without rippling. The mixture is best added after the ice cream has been churned. Make sure the mixture is well chilled before adding to the ice cream. Either:

- Transfer all the ice cream to a freezer container and pour the mixture on top. Using the handle of a small spoon or a thick skewer, gently stir the purée through the ice cream so that it forms ripples (not too much or it will blend in and not ripple).

- Or transfer half the ice cream to a freezer container and pour half the ripple mixture over the top, spreading it evenly. Carefully spoon the remaining ice cream on top, level the surface and spread the rest of the sauce evenly over it.

Storing Ices

- You can, of course, serve ices as soon as the freeze-churn process of the machine is completed (and there has been many an occasion when I have been unable to resist the temptation just to tuck in and eat it straight from the bowl in which it was made). At this stage, the mixture will be very soft and very delicious, though not firm enough to scoop.

- When the ice cream is ready, it can be kept in the ice cream machine, covered, for up to about 20 minutes. Make sure that the paddle has been removed and that the freezing unit has been switched off (otherwise the ice cream will harden too much).

- Most mixtures will benefit from 2–3 hours in the freezer, to allow the flavours to develop and settle and the ice cream to firm up to a state that is ideal for scooping and shaping.

- Transfer the ice cream from the ice cream machine into a clean freezer container – large, shallow, rigid containers are best because the contents will freeze more efficiently and the surface area will make it easy to scoop out. Seal the container well and label it with the flavour of ice cream and the date.

- Some ice creams and sorbets, and particularly those made with fresh (uncooked) fruit and yogurt, are best eaten on the day they are made – they simply taste better.

- Home-made ice creams are not suitable for keeping in the freezer for very long periods (unlike commercial ice creams that contain stabilisers and preservatives). I like to use them up within a week of being made, though if absolutely necessary they should keep for a few weeks and a maximum of two months (depending on the ingredients and the quantity being left in the freezer). The longer it is kept, the more likely it is that the texture, colour and flavour will suffer.

- To prevent bacteria from developing, do make sure that all containers and utensils are spotlessly clean, especially the parts that come into contact with the mixture.

Serving Ices

- Ice cream or sorbet that has been frozen for longer than a few hours should be allowed to soften slightly before serving, so that it's still frozen yet it's soft enough to scoop. Not only will it be easier to serve but the flavour will be better too (remember that extreme cold dulls flavour). The best way to do this is to transfer the sealed container from the freezer to your fridge about 30 minutes before serving. Alternatively, leave it at room temperature for about 15 minutes.

- Sorbet and mixtures containing alcohol are likely to soften more quickly, so you will need to keep an eye on them.

- Ice cream scoops are available in many sizes. If you like to serve ices in lots of interesting ways, you may like to have a selection, though, for most of us, a medium-size scoop is ideal for filling cones as well as for general serving. Choose the type with a spring-loaded release or one that uses the warmth of your hand to stop the ice cream sticking to the scoop.

- Alternatively, instead of a scoop, you could use a spoon that has been dipped briefly into warm water.

- Fill either the scoop or the spoon by dragging it across the surface of the ice cream or by digging it in (to create a more solid scoop of ice cream with one flat side).

- Both ice cream and sorbet can be scooped out well ahead of serving – simply arrange the scoops on trays lined with non-stick paper and pop them back into the freezer. Serve the scoops piled in a chilled glass bowl or in an ice bowl (see page 24 for instructions for making one).

- It is important to remember that ice cream that has partially or fully thawed should NEVER be refrozen, due to the danger of bacteria growth. As soon as you have finished serving, return any remaining ice cream to the freezer before it melts.

- For serving, use small plates or saucers, stemmed glasses, glass dishes or small (coffee) cups.

- If you plan to serve the ice with a dessert or some fresh fruit, use larger plates. Garnishes look better too when they are given plenty of room.

- Try hollowing out halves of fruit such as melon or pineapple and filling them with scoops of ice cream and/or sorbet; or pressing it into orange, lemon or grapefruit halves.

- Ice cream moulds make elegant desserts. Simply press the ice cream into a loaf tin and freeze it until firm. You could use a single flavour or choose two or three contrasting flavours (and colours) and layer them in the mould. To serve, wipe the outside of the tin with a hot damp cloth, invert the ice on to a flat plate and cut it into slices with a sharp knife that has been dipped in hot water (wiping it clean between each slice).

- For special occasions, dipping small balls of ice cream in chopped nuts or grated chocolate is always impressive. Or why not dip tiny ones in melted chocolate before popping them back in the freezer on a tray lined with non-stick paper? Serve them at the end of a meal, perhaps with the coffee.

- Sometimes, all an iced dessert needs to decorate it is a liberal sprinkling of icing sugar. I also like to make full use of simple things like fresh mint leaves, lemon geranium leaves, small sprigs of fresh berries (such as redcurrants or blackcurrants), soft fruit (a few raspberries always look good) and chocolate leaves or curls.

- Most ices are good served with something crisp, the obvious example being an ice cream cornet. For a more elegant presentation, try wafer biscuits or sweet biscuits like amaretti, macaroons or langues de chat.

To make an ice bowl:

1. Take two large bowls of similar shape – one should be 2.5cm/1 in or more smaller than the other.

2. Half fill the larger bowl with cold water and place the smaller bowl inside, weighing it down (cans of food are ideal for this) so that the gap between the bowls will be 2.5cm/1 in or more.

3. If you like, push some herb sprigs and/or flowers down into the water between the bowls.

4. Secure sticky tape across the tops of the bowls to prevent them moving around.

5. Place the bowls upright in the freezer on a level surface and freeze overnight or until hard.

6. To remove the ice bowl, run cold water over the outer bowl until it can be slipped off. Then you should be able to ease the ice bowl carefully off the inner bowl.

7. Return the ice bowl to the freezer until required.

8. To serve, sit the ice bowl on a folded cloth (to prevent it slipping) on a large plate (to catch the drips) and fill with scoops of ice cream and/or sorbet.

6

RECIPE REMINDERS

All the recipes in this book were tested in electrically-operated ice cream machines of various designs.

Always be sure to follow the manufacturer's instructions for preparing, using and cleaning your ice cream machine.

Servings

Each recipe gives the approximate number of servings though, obviously, this will depend on your (and your guests') appetite for ice cream.

I have tried to keep the measures manageable though the amount of ice cream you can make will depend on the capacity of your ice cream machine. You may find yourself needing to reduce quantities slightly for small machines; conversely you may be able to increase the amounts.

Ingredients

For convenience, the ingredients are listed in the order in which they are used. Though they are given in imperial as well as metric, you will find the metric measurements easier to use.

Measurements

Spoon measures are always level unless otherwise stated.

Can and carton sizes are approximate and may vary from brand to brand.

Eggs

These are usually large, unless otherwise stated. Some recipes contain raw egg whites (two of the sorbet recipes on pages 88 and 91) or partly cooked egg yolks (in the custard on page 28) – please remember that it is advisable to avoid eating these if you are a pregnant or nursing mother, elderly, very young or sick.

Recipe Methods

When giving instructions for freezing, I have assumed that the ice cream machine has been prepared following the manufacturer's instructions. To save repetition, I have assumed that the paddle and lid have been securely fitted and the mixture poured into the machine with the paddle turning.

Freezing times will depend on the quantity of mixture and its starting temperature.

Microwaves

When appropriate, I have added occasional microwave instructions. These are based on an 800W microwave. If yours is a lower wattage, you may need to cook for slightly longer. If it is a higher wattage, you may need to lower the power level slightly in order to cook for the given time.

7

THE EASIEST ICES EVER

This section is full of freezer pleasers – ices made by combining a variety of simple ingredients and throwing them into the ice cream machine for churning into velvety smooth, luscious concoctions. Sometimes, fruit is simply sweetened and mixed with cream, while other recipes involve mixing ingredients and flavourings that most of us have in our kitchen cupboards – like ready-made custard, chocolate, nuts, biscuits, vanilla extract and so on.

Everything has been chosen with taste and convenience in mind. Unlike many books about ice cream, I have tried to avoid the use of eggs and custard-making as much as possible (when I decide to make ice cream, I never seem to have the time to make a proper egg custard and allow it to cool first). This is not to say that *you* shouldn't make fresh egg custard. If time allows and you would like to replace the ready-made custard with your own fresh, home-made version, please feel free to do so. You will find a delicious recipe overleaf. The choice is yours.

Vanilla Ice Cream with Fresh Custard

This is creamy vanilla ice cream made with the real thing! The fresh egg custard here can be used to replace ready-made custard in any of the other recipes. When you have strained the mixture in step 5, save the empty vanilla pod (rinse and dry it) and use it to flavour sugar (see page 18). If you wish, the vanilla pod can be substituted with 1 tsp vanilla extract.

About 6 servings

1 vanilla pod
300ml/½ pint full cream milk
3 large egg yolks
85g/3 oz caster sugar
284ml carton double cream, chilled

1. Split the vanilla pod and, with a knife, scrape out the seeds.
2. Put the milk into a heavy-based saucepan and add the vanilla pod and the vanilla seeds.
3. Bring the mixture almost to the boil, then remove from the heat, cover and leave to stand for about 20 minutes.
4. In a bowl, beat the egg yolks with the sugar until well mixed, then stir in the milk.
5. Remove the vanilla pod and pour the mixture back into the saucepan.
6. Cook over a gentle heat, stirring continuously with a wooden spoon, until the custard thickens slightly and just coats the back of the spoon. Do not allow the mixture to boil or it will curdle. (Alternatively, cook the mixture in a bowl over a pan of gently simmering water – but do not allow the bowl to touch the water.)
7. As soon as the custard has thickened, transfer it to a clean bowl and leave to cool.
8. With a whisk, stir the cream into the custard. Cover and refrigerate until well chilled.
9. Tip the mixture into the ice cream machine and freeze according to instructions.
10. Transfer to a suitable container and freeze until required.

Quick Vanilla Ice Cream

You might decide to use the seeds from a vanilla pod in place of the vanilla extract. If so, put them into a small pan with the cream, heat through until almost boiling then cover and leave to cool completely before following the method below.

About 4–6 servings

425g carton ready-made custard, chilled
284ml carton double cream, chilled
3 level tbsp icing sugar
1 tsp vanilla extract

1. Tip the custard into a jug and add the cream.
2. Sift the icing sugar over and add the vanilla.
3. With a whisk, stir until smooth.
4. Tip the mixture into the ice cream machine and freeze according to instructions.
5. Transfer to a suitable container and freeze until required.

Chocolate Ice Cream

"Velvety and luxurious" was the unanimous verdict on this ice cream. I have used a good quality chocolate (50 per cent or more cocoa solids) but you could use a good quality cocoa powder instead. Simply dissolve 2 tablespoonfuls of cocoa powder in a small amount of boiling water to make a smooth cream and add it.

About 4–6 servings

140g/5 oz plain chocolate
2 level tbsp muscovado sugar
284ml carton double cream, chilled
425g carton ready-made custard, chilled

1. Break the chocolate into a small pan and add the sugar and cream. (Alternatively, put the chocolate, sugar and cream into a suitable bowl.)
2. Heat gently, stirring frequently and without boiling, until the sugar has dissolved and the chocolate has melted. Cover and leave to cool. (Or microwave on Medium, stirring occasionally, until the sugar has dissolved and the chocolate has melted.)
3. Add the custard to the chocolate mixture and, with a whisk, stir until smooth.
4. Cover and chill in the refrigerator for about 30 minutes.
5. Tip the mixture into the ice cream machine and freeze according to instructions.
6. Transfer to a suitable container and freeze until required.

Fresh Lemon Ice

This fresh-tasting ice is, I think, best served on the day it is made. This version is silky smooth and rich. For a lighter version, use a 200g carton of Greek yogurt in place of the cream. Either way, try serving it with your favourite lemon cake (either freshly baked or gently warmed through).

About 6 servings

405g can skimmed sweetened condensed milk
142ml carton double cream, chilled
4 lemons

1. Tip the condensed milk into a jug and add the cream.
2. Cut the lemons in half and squeeze their juice. Strain the juice into the jug.
3. With a whisk, stir until the mixture is smooth.
4. Cover and chill in the refrigerator for about 30 minutes.
5. Tip the mixture into the ice cream machine and freeze according to instructions.
6. Transfer to a suitable container and freeze until required.

Blackberry and Elderflower Ice

This ice is such a pretty colour and, if you can lay your hands on some fresh brambles, the flavour will be spectacular. It's delicious made with raspberries too. Sometimes I serve it with a little extra elderflower cordial drizzled over the top.

About 6 servings

225g/8 oz blackberries
1 tbsp sugar
284ml carton double cream, chilled
8 tbsp elderflower cordial
142ml carton whipping cream, chilled

1. Put the blackberries into a small saucepan and add the sugar. Heat gently, stirring occasionally, until the juice runs from the fruit and the mixture comes to the boil. Simmer gently for 2–3 minutes until the blackberries are very soft. (Alternatively, put the blackberries and sugar into a suitable bowl and microwave on High for 2–3 minutes or until the fruit is very soft.)
2. Press the blackberry mixture through a sieve and discard the seeds. Leave the purée to cool then cover and refrigerate for about 30 minutes or until well chilled.
3. Meanwhile, tip the double cream into a jug, add the elderflower cordial and stir until smooth. Cover and chill for 20–30 minutes.
4. Stir the blackberry purée into the elderflower mixture until smooth.
5. Tip the whipping cream into a bowl and whisk until soft peaks are formed.
6. Gently fold the whipped cream into the blackberry mixture.
7. Tip the mixture into the ice cream machine and freeze according to instructions.
8. Transfer to a suitable container and freeze until required.

Cranberry and Orange Ice

I like to make this over the Christmas holiday when serving cranberries seems particularly appropriate. It's lovely with hot Christmas pudding or mince pies.

This recipe uses a jar of cranberry sauce. If you use your own home-made sauce, taste the final mixture before freezing to check that it is sweet enough – if not, whisk in a little clear honey or sifted icing sugar.

About 6 servings

125g/4½ oz plain Greek yogurt, chilled
425g carton ready-made custard, chilled
195g jar cranberry sauce
3 tbsp fine-cut marmalade

1. Tip the yogurt and custard into a large jug and, with a whisk, stir well.
2. Add the cranberry sauce and marmalade and whisk until well mixed.
3. Cover and chill in the refrigerator for about 30 minutes.
4. Tip the mixture into the ice cream machine and freeze according to instructions.
5. Transfer to a suitable container and freeze until required.

Bramble Ice Cream

I like to use brambles because they have such an intense flavour and impart such a beautiful colour. You could of course use cultivated blackberries instead. For speed, use ready-made custard from a can or carton.

About 6 servings

350g/12 oz brambles, rinsed and drained
85g/3 oz caster or granulated sugar
284ml carton double cream
225g/8 oz ready-made custard

1. Put the brambles into a saucepan and sprinkle the sugar over. Heat gently, stirring occasionally, until the juices run from the brambles and come to the boil. Simmer gently for about 5 minutes until the fruit is very soft. (Alternatively, put the brambles and sugar into a suitable bowl and microwave on High for about 3 minutes or until the fruit is very soft.)
2. Press the bramble mixture through a sieve and discard the seeds. Leave the purée to cool then refrigerate until chilled.
3. Tip the cream into a jug and add the custard and bramble purée.
4. Cover and chill for about 30 minutes.
5. Tip the mixture into the ice cream machine and freeze according to instructions.
6. Transfer to a suitable container and freeze until required.

Strawberry Pavlova Ripple

Here, the ingredients for Eton Mess (a dessert made with crushed meringues, thick cream and fresh strawberries) are put together and frozen to make the most wonderful ice cream.

About 6 servings

450g/1 lb ripe strawberries
3 tbsp caster sugar
284ml carton double cream, chilled
½ tsp vanilla extract
4 meringue nests or about 60g/2¼ oz meringues

1. Remove the leafy hulls from the strawberries.
2. Put the strawberries into a food processor or blender, add the sugar and blend until smooth. Alternatively, mash them on a large plate, making sure that all the juices are retained and the mixture is fairly smooth.
3. Tip the cream into a jug. Add the vanilla extract and half the strawberry purée. Crumble in the meringue nests and stir well.
4. Refrigerate for 15–20 minutes until the meringues have dissolved and the mixture is well chilled.
5. Tip the mixture into the ice cream machine and freeze according to instructions.
6. Transfer to a suitable container and pour the remaining strawberry purée over the top. With a small spoon or a skewer, gently stir the purée through the ice cream so that it forms ripples.
7. Freeze until required.

Blackberry and Vanilla Ice Cream

Use brambles if you can get them – for their intense flavour. It makes a good accompaniment to warm apple pie or apple cake.

About 6 servings

175g/6 oz blackberries, rinsed and drained
40g/1½ oz caster or granulated sugar
284ml carton whipping cream, chilled
1 tsp vanilla extract
225g/8 oz ready-made custard, chilled

1. Put the blackberries into a small saucepan and sprinkle the sugar over. Heat gently, stirring occasionally, until the juices run from the blackberries and come to the boil. Simmer gently for 2–3 minutes until the fruit is very soft. (Alternatively, put the blackberries and sugar into a suitable bowl and microwave on High for about 2 minutes or until the fruit is very soft.)
2. Press the blackberry mixture through a sieve and discard the seeds. Leave the purée to cool then refrigerate until chilled.
3. Tip the cream into a large jug and whisk until sufficiently thickened to form ribbons on the surface (it should not form peaks). Stir in the vanilla, custard and blackberry purée.
4. Tip the mixture into the ice cream machine and freeze according to instructions.
5. Transfer to a suitable container and freeze until required.

Mango Ice Cream

This delightful recipe was given to me by my good friend and talented chef, Simon Kealy. I have simply adjusted the quantities to make them suitable for standard-size ice cream machines. I have also made the recipe using 400g/14 oz canned mango purée in place of the fresh mangoes. The glucose is optional – it helps to prevent the ice cream from setting too hard (*essential in Simon's restaurant*).

About 4–6 servings

115g/4 oz caster sugar
2 large ripe mangoes
1 small lime
200ml/7 fl oz double cream, chilled
1 tsp glucose syrup

1. Put the sugar in a small pan with 2 tbsp water and heat gently until the sugar has dissolved. (Alternatively, put the sugar and water into a microwaveable bowl and microwave on Medium for 1–2 minutes or until the sugar has dissolved.) Remove from the heat and leave to cool.
2. Meanwhile, with a sharp knife, cut the mangoes and remove their stones. Remove the flesh from the skin and put it into a food processor or blender. Squeeze the juice from the lime and add to the mango. Purée until smooth.
3. With a whisk, stir together the mango purée, cream, glucose and cooled sugar syrup.
4. Cover and chill for about 30 minutes.
5. Tip the mixture into the ice cream machine and freeze according to instructions.
6. Transfer to a suitable container and freeze until required.

Banana and Passion Fruit Ice

This is a wonderful way to use up those really ripe bananas with black skins. The passion fruit should be ripe too – look for wrinkly skins.

About 6 servings

3 or 4 ripe bananas, about 400g/14 oz total peeled weight
2 passion fruit
425g carton custard
1 tbsp clear honey
1 tbsp lemon juice
½ tsp vanilla extract

1. Peel the bananas and break them into a food processor or blender.
2. Halve the passion fruit and, with a spoon, scoop out the seeds and juice straight into the processor.
3. Add the remaining ingredients and purée until smooth (the passion fruit seeds should still remain whole).
4. Tip the mixture into a large jug, cover and refrigerate for at least 30 minutes or until well chilled.
5. Tip the mixture into the ice cream machine and freeze according to instructions.
6. Transfer to a suitable container and freeze until required.

Strawberries and Clotted Cream

"The strawberriest ice cream I have ever tasted!" was the verdict of my daughter Lindsay. The flavour, she said, took her back to the pick-your-own farm in Ockley where she and her sister used to gather (and eat) as many sunshine-warm strawberries as they could.

The pungent sweetness of the balsamic vinegar really brings out the flavour of the fresh strawberries.

About 4–6 servings

250g/9 oz ripe strawberries
55g/2 oz caster sugar
2 tsp balsamic vinegar
225g/8 oz clotted cream, chilled

1. Remove the leafy hulls from the strawberries.
2. Put the strawberries into a food processor or blender and add the sugar and balsamic vinegar. Blend until smooth.
3. Add the cream to the strawberry mixture and blend until smooth.
4. Cover and refrigerate the mixture for about 30 minutes or until well chilled.
5. Tip the mixture into the ice cream machine and freeze according to instructions.
6. Transfer to a suitable container and freeze until required.

Cherry Ice Cream

Depending on the capacity of your ice cream machine, you may need to freeze this mixture in two batches. Try it using flavours other than cherry too – such as apricot, peach or rhubarb compote.

About 6–8 servings

600g jar cherry compote
4 tbsp caster sugar
284ml double cream, chilled
2–3 tbsp cherry liqueur (optional)

1. Tip the cherry compote into a large jug and stir in the sugar. Stir in the remaining ingredients.
2. Cover and refrigerate for 30 minutes or until well chilled.
3. Tip the mixture into the ice cream machine and freeze according to instructions.
4. Transfer to a suitable container and freeze until required.

Apricot and Almond Ice

Serve with crisp biscuits such as amaretti.

About 6–8 servings

397g can condensed milk
410g can apricot halves in fruit juice
¼ tsp almond extract
40g/1½ oz blanched almonds

1. Tip the condensed milk into a food processor or blender and add the apricots and their juice and the almond extract. Purée until smooth.
2. Cover and chill in the refrigerator for about 30 minutes.
3. Meanwhile, chop the almonds and put them into a dry frying pan. Over medium heat, toast them, stirring occasionally, until golden brown. Tip on to a plate and leave to cool.
4. Tip the chilled apricot mixture into the ice cream machine and freeze according to instructions.
5. Add the toasted almonds during the final minute or two of churning.
6. Transfer to a suitable container and freeze until required.

Mandarin and Chocolate Ice

The delicate flavour of the mandarin combines well with a small amount of chocolate. My tasters think the texture of this ice is best (smoothest) on the day it's made.

About 6 servings

212g can mandarin segments in syrup
200g carton, plain Greek yogurt, chilled
142ml carton double cream, chilled
4 generous tbsp chocolate hazelnut spread
3 tbsp cream liqueur
1 tbsp icing sugar

1. Put the mandarin segments and their syrup into a food processor or blender. Add the yogurt, cream, chocolate spread, liqueur and sugar. Blend until smooth.
2. Cover and refrigerate the mixture for about 30 minutes or until well chilled.
3. Tip the mixture into the ice cream machine and freeze according to instructions.
4. Transfer to a suitable container and freeze until required.

Vanilla and Chocolate Chip Ice Cream

This combination was devised by my young nieces and is now a favourite with adults and children alike. For the best flavour, make sure you use natural vanilla (extract or essence) and not an artificial flavouring.

About 4–6 servings

284ml carton double cream, chilled
250g/9 oz low fat natural yogurt, chilled
6 level tbsp icing sugar
1 tsp vanilla extract
100g packet chocolate chips

1. Tip the cream into a jug and add the yogurt.
2. Sift the icing sugar over the cream and yogurt and add the vanilla.
3. With a whisk, stir until smooth.
4. Tip the mixture into the ice cream machine and freeze according to instructions.
5. Add the chocolate chips during the final minute or two of churning.
6. Transfer to a suitable container and freeze until required.

Muscovado and Rum Ice

A rich and creamy ice with an almost butterscotch flavour. It's particularly good served with warm poached pears or hot apple pie.

About 6 servings

284ml carton double cream, chilled
300g/10½ oz plain Greek yogurt, chilled
115g/4 oz muscovado sugar
2 tbsp dark rum
1½ tsp vanilla extract

1. Tip the cream into a jug and add the yogurt and muscovado sugar.
2. With a whisk, stir well.
3. Cover and refrigerate for about 30 minutes, by which time the sugar will have dissolved.
4. Add the rum and vanilla and stir well.
5. Tip the mixture into the ice cream machine and freeze according to instructions.
6. Transfer to a suitable container and freeze until required.

Amaretti Ice

It can't get much simpler than this – just three ingredients producing a velvety texture and a delightful bitter-almond flavour. I like to serve this just as it is (maybe with extra amaretti biscuits), with pears poached in syrup, with warm pear tart or with any dessert made with apricots.

About 6 servings

500g carton ready-made custard, chilled
250g/9 oz plain Greek yogurt, chilled
115g/4 oz amaretti or macaroon biscuits

1. Tip the custard and yogurt into a large jug and, with a whisk, stir well.
2. Crush the amaretti biscuits into fine crumbs (use a processor or blender or simply pop them into a plastic food bag and crush gently with a rolling pin).
3. Stir the biscuit crumbs into the custard-and-yogurt mixture.
4. Tip the mixture into the ice cream machine and freeze according to instructions.
5. Transfer to a suitable container and freeze until required.

Rhubarb and Custard Ice

A traditional combination is transformed into a delicious ice cream using the most convenient ingredients. Check that the quantity will fit in your ice cream machine – you may need to reduce the quantities or freeze it in two batches.

About 8–10 servings

600g jar rhubarb compote
425g carton custard
1 small orange

1. Tip the rhubarb compote into a jug and add the custard.
2. With a whisk, stir until smooth.
3. Finely grate the zest from the orange and stir into the rhubarb mixture.
4. Cover and chill for about 1 hour.
5. Tip the mixture into the ice cream machine and freeze according to instructions.
6. Transfer to a suitable container and freeze until required.

Rum and Raisin Ice Cream

Here's a rich and creamy blend that has always been a favourite with most of my family. If the ice cream is frozen for longer than a day, the rum keeps it just soft enough to serve straight from the freezer.

About 6–8 servings

85g/3 oz raisins
3 tbsp dark rum
450g carton custard
284ml carton double cream, chilled
2 tbsp caster sugar

1. Put the raisins into a small bowl and sprinkle with the rum. Cover and leave to stand for several hours or, if time allows, overnight.
2. Tip the custard into a jug and add the cream and sugar. Stir well.
3. Chill the mixture in the refrigerator for 20–30 minutes.
4. Stir the raisins and rum into the custard mixture.
5. Tip the mixture into the ice cream machine and freeze according to instructions.
6. Transfer to a suitable container and freeze until required.

Chunky Pecan and Maple Ice Cream

A sweet concoction that is wonderful served with hot apple pie, with Butterscotch or Coffee Caramel Sauce (see pages 107 and 114). It's also good served just as it is, with or without cones or wafers. Do use real maple syrup and not syrup that is simply flavoured with maple.

About 6 servings

284ml carton double cream, chilled
284ml carton single cream, chilled
6 tbsp maple syrup
100g/3½ oz pecan halves

1. Tip both cartons of cream into a jug and add the maple syrup.
2. With a whisk, stir until smooth.
3. Cover and chill for about 30 minutes.
4. Meanwhile, finely chop the pecan halves.
5. Tip the mixture into the ice cream machine and freeze according to instructions.
6. Add the chopped pecans during the final minute or two of churning.
7. Transfer to a suitable container and freeze until required.

Coconut Ice

This recipe includes desiccated coconut and a caramel-like, sweet coconut spread that is usually obtainable from oriental supermarkets. If you prefer a smooth ice cream, try the Coconut and Lime Ice Cream on page 52.

About 6 servings

400ml can coconut milk
142ml carton double cream, chilled
4 tbsp sweet coconut spread (see note above)
25g/1 oz desiccated coconut

1. Tip the coconut milk into a jug and add the cream and coconut spread.
2. With a whisk, stir until smooth.
3. Stir in the desiccated coconut.
4. Cover and chill for about 30 minutes.
5. Tip the mixture into the ice cream machine and freeze according to instructions.
6. Transfer to a suitable container and freeze until required.

Almond and Chocolate Raisin Ice Cream

This recipe was devised by my nieces, Megan and Siân, who come to stay with us every summer. The chocolate-covered raisins add interesting chewy bits to a simple almond-flavoured ice cream.

About 6 servings

25g/1 oz blanched almonds
284ml carton double cream, chilled
250g/9 oz low fat natural yogurt, chilled
6 level tbsp icing sugar
½ tsp almond extract
100g/3½ oz milk chocolate raisins

1. Chop the almonds finely. Put them into a small frying pan and toast, stirring occasionally, until golden brown (take care not to let them get too brown and burn). Transfer them to a plate and leave to cool.
2. Tip the cream into a jug and add the yogurt.
3. Sift the icing sugar over the cream and yogurt and add the almond extract.
4. With a whisk, stir until smooth.
5. Cover and chill for 20-30 minutes.
6. Tip the mixture into the ice cream machine and freeze according to instructions.
7. Add the chocolate raisins and toasted almonds during the final minute or two of churning.
8. Transfer to a suitable container and freeze until required.

Pistachio Ice Cream

Pistachio ice cream is an all-time favourite of my husband Huw. He prefers it scooped into a good quality cone; I like it particularly with some fresh summer fruits alongside.

About 6 servings

115g/4 oz shelled pistachios
55g/2 oz golden caster sugar
284ml carton single cream, chilled
250g carton custard

1. Put the pistachios into a food processor and add the sugar. Process until finely ground.
2. Tip the cream into a jug and add the custard and pistachio mixture.
3. With a whisk, stir well.
4. Cover and chill for about 30 minutes by which time the sugar should have dissolved.
5. Tip the mixture into the ice cream machine and freeze according to instructions.
6. Transfer to a suitable container and freeze until required.

Coconut and Lime Ice Cream

The freshly squeezed lime juice really complements the flavour of the coconut. For the best texture, serve it on the day it is made. If you like pieces of coconut in your ice cream, try the recipe for Coconut Ice on page 49 which includes desiccated coconut.

About 6 servings

Two 200ml cartons coconut cream
142ml carton double cream, chilled
85g/3 oz caster sugar
1 lime

1. Tip the coconut cream into a jug and add the cream and sugar.
2. With a whisk, stir well.
3. Halve the lime and squeeze about 2 tbsp lime juice into the coconut mixture.
4. Cover and chill for about 30 minutes by which time the sugar should have dissolved.
5. Tip the mixture into the ice cream machine and freeze according to instructions.
6. Transfer to a suitable container and freeze until required.

Pear and Amaretti Ice

This recipe was created in an attempt to use up small quantities of cream, fromage frais and amaretti biscuits – all left over from a dinner party the night before. The result is a light ice with a delicate flavour. For me, it's best made and eaten on the same day. Instead of fromage frais, you could use thick yogurt or extra cream.

About 6 servings

400g can pear halves or quarters in fruit juice
200g/7 oz fromage frais
142ml carton double cream
2 tbsp icing sugar
55g/2 oz amaretti biscuits

1. Tip the pears and their juice into a food processor or blender.
2. Add the fromage frais, cream, sugar and biscuits.
3. Blend until smooth.
4. Cover and refrigerate for about 30 minutes until chilled.
5. Tip the mixture into the ice cream machine and freeze according to instructions.
6. Transfer to a suitable container and freeze until required.

Fig and Mascarpone Ice

The idea for this mixture came to me one evening when I was serving one of my favourite desserts – fresh figs split open, filled with mascarpone cheese, drizzled with honey and flashed under a hot grill. When they are in season I like to use a mixture of really fresh ripe figs together with a few ready-to-eat dried ones. For year-round convenience, the recipe uses canned figs. Make sure you use honey with a good flavour, such as orange blossom. Serve it in small scoops (it's quite rich) just as it is; or it's particularly good with any dessert or biscuit containing almonds.

About 4–6 servings

410g can figs in syrup
250g carton mascarpone cheese
3 tbsp clear honey
2 tsp fresh lemon juice

1. Drain the figs and remove the tough ends of their stalks.
2. Put the figs in a food processor or blender and add the mascarpone, honey and lemon juice. Blend until smooth.
3. Cover and refrigerate for about 30 minutes until chilled.
4. Tip the mixture into the ice cream machine and freeze according to instructions.
5. Transfer to a suitable container and freeze until required.

Chocolate Honeycomb Ice Cream

This was created to use one of those multi packs of chocolate bars. Feel free to replace the fromage frais with cream (double, single or whipping) or Greek yogurt. If you decide to omit the almond liqueur, the ice cream is probably best eaten soon after it is made. I serve it topped with an extra sprinkling of chocolate honeycomb, which means I either reserve a little of the main ingredient or buy an extra bar!

About 6 servings

4 chocolate honeycomb bars, about 150g/5½ oz in total
284ml carton double cream, chilled
200g carton fromage frais, chilled
3 tbsp almond liqueur, such as amaretto (optional)

1. Crush the honeycomb bars into small crumbs – I do this by putting them into a freezer bag and crushing them with a rolling pin.
2. Tip the cream into a jug and add the fromage frais and liqueur (if using). With a whisk, stir until smooth.
3. Stir in the chocolate honeycomb crumbs.
4. Cover and refrigerate for about 30 minutes until chilled.
5. Tip the mixture into the ice cream machine and freeze according to instructions.
6. Transfer to a suitable container and freeze until required.

Toasted Apple and Cinnamon Ice

This creamy ice is lovely served with Maple Sauce (page 111,) warm ginger cake, spiced biscuits or lightly cooked blackberries.

About 6 servings

About 300g/10 oz sharp eating or sweet cooking apples
25g/1 oz butter
55g/2 oz light muscovado sugar
½ tsp ground cinnamon
425g carton custard
150ml/¼ pt natural low-fat yogurt, chilled
½ tsp vanilla extract

1. Peel and core the apples and cut into small pieces.
2. Heat the butter in a non-stick frying pan, add the sugar and stir until dissolved.
3. Stir the apples into the butter and sugar mixture and add the cinnamon.
4. Cook for 5–10 minutes, stirring occasionally, until softened, golden brown and caramelised. Remove from the heat.
5. Tip the custard into a jug and add the yogurt and vanilla. With a whisk, stir until smooth.
6. Add the apples to the custard mixture, scraping out every last scrap of flavour from the pan.
7. Cover and refrigerate for about 30 minutes until chilled.
8. Tip the mixture into the ice cream machine and freeze according to instructions.
9. Transfer to a suitable container and freeze until required.

Golden Fig Ice with Rum

This is an iced version of an Italian dessert that was served to me one summer. It's quite rich so serve it in small scoops with warm lemon cake and desserts flavoured with apricots. It's also good made with orange liqueur instead of rum.

About 6–8 servings

150g ready-to-eat dried figs
250g carton mascarpone cheese
200g carton Greek yogurt
2 tbsp light muscovado sugar
2 tbsp dark rum

1. Put the figs into a food processor or blender. Add the mascarpone cheese, yogurt, sugar and rum. Blend until smooth, scraping down the sides when necessary.
2. Cover and refrigerate for about 30 minutes until chilled.
3. Tip the mixture into the ice cream machine and freeze according to instructions.
4. Transfer to a suitable container and freeze until required.

Chocolate Caramel Crunch

Rich and wickedly indulgent, but oh so good!

About 4–6 servings

Two 50g bars chocolate caramel
142ml carton double cream
425g carton custard
Two 45g packs milk chocolate finger twirls or flakes

1. Break the caramel bars into squares and put into a small saucepan with the cream. (Alternatively, put them into a microwaveable bowl.)
2. Heat gently, stirring, until the caramel has dissolved and the mixture is smooth. (Or microwave on High for 1–1½ minutes, stirring occasionally, until the caramel has dissolved and the mixture is smooth.)
3. Remove from the heat and, with a whisk, stir the caramel mixture into the custard.
4. Cover and refrigerate for about 30 minutes or until well chilled.
5. Tip the mixture into the ice cream machine and freeze according to instructions.
6. Transfer to a suitable container.
7. Crumble the chocolate fingers and gently stir into the ice cream.
8. Freeze until required.

Caramel Walnut Ice Cream

Small servings are in order here – the mixture is deliciously rich. For a lighter version, replace the cream with yogurt.

About 4–6 servings

Four 50g bars chocolate caramel
400ml/14 fl oz milk
1 tbsp good quality instant coffee granules
284ml carton double cream
1 tbsp lemon juice
50g/1¾ oz walnut pieces

1. Break the chocolate bars into squares and put into a pan with the milk and coffee. (Alternatively, put them into a microwaveable bowl.)
2. Heat gently, stirring, until the chocolate has melted, the caramel has dissolved and the sauce is smooth. (Or microwave on High for about 1½ minutes, stirring occasionally, until the chocolate has melted, the caramel has dissolved and the sauce is smooth.)
3. Remove from the heat and stir in the cream and lemon juice.
4. Chop the walnuts and stir into the caramel mixture.
5. Leave to cool then cover and chill for about 30 minutes.
6. Tip the mixture into the ice cream machine and freeze according to instructions.
7. Transfer to a suitable container and freeze until required.

Christmas Pudding Ice Cream

Possibly my favourite way to use up the remnants of the festive pud. Serve it with Berry Fruit Sauce (page 112), Orange and Lemon Sauce (page 105) or The Simplest Apricot Sauce (page 106). The Welsh fruit cake called Bara Brith makes an excellent alternative to Christmas Pudding – how about Bara Brith and Whisky Ice Cream?

About 6–8 servings

284ml carton double cream, chilled
500g carton ready-made custard
2 tbsp brandy or rum
About 225g/8 oz Christmas pudding

1. Tip the cream into a large jug. With a whisk, stir in the custard and brandy/rum.
2. Cover and refrigerate for about 30 minutes or until well chilled.
3. Tip the mixture into the ice cream machine and freeze according to instructions.
4. Meanwhile, crumble or chop the Christmas pudding into very small pieces.
5. Transfer to a suitable container and stir in the crumbled pudding.
6. Freeze until required.

Boozy Turkish Cream

Top each serving of this scented ice with a few chopped pistachio nuts or toasted, slivered almonds.

About 4–6 servings

200g carton Greek yogurt, chilled
284ml carton double cream, chilled
85g/3 oz caster sugar
4 tbsp orange liqueur
2 tbsp orange-flower water
2 tbsp rosewater
1 small lime

1. Tip the yogurt and cream into a large jug. With a whisk, stir in the sugar, liqueur, orange-flower water and rosewater.
2. Halve the lime and squeeze its juice. Stir into the jug.
3. Cover and refrigerate for 20–30 minutes or until well chilled.
4. Tip the mixture into the ice cream machine and freeze according to instructions.
5. Transfer to a suitable container and freeze until required.

White Chocolate and Ratafia Ice

A creamy rich dessert that is delicious served with The Simplest Apricot Sauce (the one made with canned apricot halves on page 106). After churning, I usually freeze the ice cream in a loaf tin. When it is time to serve, I turn it out on to a flat plate and press extra crushed ratafias over the top and sides. Then it's ready to slice.

About 8 servings

175g/6 oz white chocolate
142ml carton single cream
284ml carton double cream, chilled
3 tbsp almond liqueur
50g/1¾ oz ratafia biscuits

1. Break the chocolate into squares and put into a small saucepan with the single cream. (Alternatively, put them into a microwaveable bowl.)
2. Heat gently, stirring occasionally, until the chocolate has just melted and the mixture is smooth. (Or microwave on Medium, stirring occasionally, until the chocolate has just melted and the mixture is smooth.)
3. Remove from the heat and stir in the double cream and liqueur.
4. Crush the biscuits into crumbs and stir in.
5. Transfer to a jug, cover and refrigerate for about 30 minutes or until well chilled.
6. Tip the mixture into the ice cream machine and freeze according to instructions.
7. Transfer to a suitable container and freeze until required.

Brown Bread Ice Cream

A favourite in my family, particularly when served with just-cooked bread and butter pudding! Make it extra special by replacing the vanilla extract with a couple of tablespoonfuls of whisky or rum.

About 4–6 servings

100g/3½ oz wholemeal breadcrumbs
100g/3½ oz demerara sugar
284ml carton double cream
284ml carton single cream
1 tsp vanilla extract

1. Preheat the oven to 200°C, 400°F or Gas 6.
2. Combine the breadcrumbs with the sugar and spread the mixture on a greased baking tray. Put into the hot oven for about 10 minutes, stirring occasionally, or until crisp and golden. Leave to cool completely.
3. Tip all the cream into a large jug and stir in the vanilla extract and the cooled crumbs.
4. Cover and refrigerate for about 30 minutes or until well chilled.
5. Tip the mixture into the ice cream machine and freeze according to instructions.
6. Transfer to a suitable container and freeze until required.

Kulfi

I usually freeze this Indian ice cream in individual moulds for serving at the end of a spicy meal. This version uses pistachio nuts. Serve it straight from the freezer topped with an extra sprinkling of chopped nuts.

About 6 servings

175g/6 oz pistachio nuts
284ml carton double cream
300ml/½ pint full cream milk
3 tbsp caster sugar
¼ tsp ground cardamom
½ tsp vanilla extract

1. Put the pistachio nuts into a food processor or blender and buzz until very finely chopped.
2. Tip the ground nuts into a large saucepan and stir in the cream, milk, sugar and cardamom. (Alternatively, put them into a suitable large bowl.)
3. Bring slowly to the boil, stirring, then bubble gently for 3–5 minutes until thickened, stirring all the time to prevent the mixture catching on the bottom of the pan. (Alternatively, microwave on High until the mixture just comes to the boil, then continue cooking for 2–3 minutes until the mixture has thickened.)
4. Remove from the heat and stir in the vanilla. Leave to cool.
5. Cover and refrigerate for about 30 minutes or until well chilled.
6. Tip the mixture into the ice cream machine and freeze according to instructions.
7. Transfer to a suitable container or into individual moulds and freeze until required.
8. Serve sprinkled with the remaining pistachio nuts.

Coffee and Walnut Ice Cream

Use a good quality instant coffee.

About 6 servings

3 tbsp good quality instant coffee granules
150g/5½ oz golden caster sugar
55g/2 oz walnuts
284ml carton double cream

1. Put the coffee and sugar into a large jug, pour over 300ml/½ pint boiling water. Stir until the coffee and sugar have dissolved. Leave to cool.
2. Finely chop the walnuts.
3. Stir the walnuts and cream into the cooled mixture.
4. Cover and refrigerate for about 30 minutes or until well chilled.
5. Tip the mixture into the ice cream machine and freeze according to instructions.
6. Transfer to a suitable container and freeze until required.

Ginger Ice Cream

I adore this ice, which is studded with pieces of ginger. Serve it just as it is with crisp biscuits or wafers, or with hot steamed puddings or warm cakes such as parkin. For a really smooth result, purée the mixture in a food processor or blender before transferring it to the ice cream machine.

About 6 servings

450g jar ginger preserve
500g carton Greek yogurt, chilled
150ml carton double cream, chilled

1. Tip the ginger preserve into a large jug.
2. With a whisk, stir in the yogurt and cream.
3. Cover and refrigerate for about 30 minutes or until well chilled.
4. Tip the mixture into the ice cream machine and freeze according to instructions.
5. Transfer to a suitable container and freeze until required.

Tutti Frutti Rice Ice

I made this a special treat for my father, who just loves canned rice pudding. The fruit is soaked in orange juice but you could use brandy or rum in its place.

About 6–8 servings

50g/1¾ oz glacé cherries
50g/1¾ oz candied peel
25g/1 oz angelica
50g/1¾ oz raisins or sultanas
75ml/2½ fl oz orange juice
425g can rice pudding
284ml carton single cream
100g/3½ oz golden caster sugar

1. Finely chop the cherries, candied peel and angelica and put them in a small bowl. Add the raisins. Pour the orange juice over, cover and leave to stand for at least 1 hour.
2. Tip the rice pudding into a large jug. With a whisk, stir in the remaining ingredients.
3. Cover and refrigerate for about 30 minutes or until well chilled.
4. Tip the mixture into the ice cream machine and freeze according to instructions.
5. Add the fruit and juices for the final minute or two of churning.
6. Transfer to a suitable container and freeze until required.

Tomato and Basil Ice Cream

"A savoury ice cream is a complete surprise, but it will amaze and delight," says my good friend and colleague Norma Miller, who kindly contributed this recipe. She recommends serving it sliced or diced with crisp, wafer-thin savoury biscuits.

About 4–6 servings

300ml carton double cream, lightly whipped
500g carton passata (sieved Italian tomatoes)
2 tbsp vodka, gin or dry vermouth, or water
3 spring onions, very finely chopped
2 handfuls of finely chopped fresh basil leaves
1 tbsp Worcestershire sauce
salt and white pepper

1. Put the first six ingredients into a bowl and gently mix together. Season to taste with salt and pepper.
2. Cover and refrigerate for about 30 minutes or until well chilled.
3. Tip the mixture into the ice cream machine and freeze according to instructions.
4. Transfer to a suitable container and freeze until required.

8

ICED YOGURTS

Quick to make and light in texture, these ices use plain (natural) or flavoured yogurt as their base. Because of their lower fat content, yogurt ices tend to freeze harder than those based on cream or custard and I prefer to serve them on the day they are made. If they have been frozen for longer, you will probably need to allow plenty of time for them to soften up – so take them out of the freezer and put into the refrigerator about 30–40 minutes before serving.

Many of the other recipes in this book can be made with yogurt in place of the cream or the custard. Creamy Greek yogurt generally produces the best results.

Banana Yogurt Ice

Use really ripe bananas for the best flavour. Delicious served with Maple or Butterscotch Sauce *(see pages 111 and 107).*

About 6 servings

500g carton plain Greek yogurt, chilled
125g/4½ oz icing sugar
3 medium-to-large bananas

1. Tip the yogurt into a jug and sift the icing sugar over the top.
2. With a whisk, stir until smooth.
3. Peel the bananas and mash them (with a fork on a large plate).
4. Stir the banana mash into the yogurt mixture.
5. Cover and chill in the refrigerator for about 30 minutes.
6. Tip the mixture into the ice cream machine and freeze according to instructions.
7. Transfer to a suitable container and freeze until required.

Ginger and Rhubarb Yogurt Ice

Turn a pot of yogurt into something special! I like to use an organic rhubarb yogurt which is not too sweet. This yogurt ice goes well with hot fruit pies. Try the recipe using other flavours too – such as raspberry or apricot.

About 4–6 servings

450g carton rhubarb yogurt, chilled
142ml carton single cream, chilled
4 tbsp syrup from a jar of stem ginger
3 pieces stem ginger, drained

1. Tip the yogurt into a jug and add the cream and ginger syrup.
2. Chop the stem ginger into very small pieces and add to the jug.
3. With a whisk, stir until well mixed.
4. Cover and chill for 20–30 minutes.
5. Tip the mixture into the ice cream machine and freeze according to instructions.
6. Transfer to a suitable container and freeze until required.

Roasted Apple and Maple Ice

I particularly like to serve this light ice with fresh ripe figs or warm orange cake. In my opinion, it's at its best on the day it is made.

About 6 servings

About 300g/10 oz sharp eating or sweet cooking apples
25g/1 oz butter
2 tbsp light muscovado sugar
Pinch of ground cinnamon
500g carton natural low-fat yogurt
4 tbsp maple syrup

1. Peel and core the apples and cut into small pieces.
2. Heat the butter in a non-stick frying pan, add the sugar and cinnamon and stir until dissolved.
3. Stir the apples into the butter and sugar mixture.
4. Cook for 5–10 minutes, stirring occasionally, until softened, golden brown and caramelised. Remove from the heat.
5. Tip the yogurt into a jug and add the maple syrup. With a whisk, stir until smooth.
6. Add the apples to the yogurt mixture, scraping out every last scrap of flavour from the pan.
7. Cover and refrigerate for about 30 minutes until chilled.
8. Tip the mixture into the ice cream machine and freeze according to instructions.
9. Transfer to a suitable container and freeze until required.

Strawberry Yogurt Ice

Chef, Simon Kealy, shared this recipe with me. Simon serves this summer treat at his restaurant in Monmouthshire. It's fresh tasting and really fruity.

About 4 servings

1 unwaxed lemon
500g/1 lb 2 oz ripe strawberries
125g/4½ oz caster sugar
200g/7 oz full cream yogurt
4 tbsp milk

1. Finely grate the zest from the lemon and squeeze out 1 tbsp juice.
2. Remove the leafy hulls from the strawberries.
3. Put the strawberries into a food processor or blender and blend until smooth.
4. Add the 1 tbsp lemon juice and half the sugar and blend again.
5. With a whisk, combine the yogurt with the remaining sugar, the milk and lemon zest. Stir in the strawberry purée.
6. Cover and refrigerate for about 30 minutes or until well chilled.
7. Tip the mixture into the ice cream machine and freeze according to instructions.
8. Transfer to a suitable container and freeze until required.

Iced Lemon Meringue

Sweet yet sharp, this ice contains chunks of crunchy meringue. It's good served in brandy snap baskets. Home-made lemon curd gives the best flavour, otherwise use a good quality (luxury) brand. The Greek yogurt gives a slightly grainy texture, which I like, though you could of course replace it with cream – single, whipping or double.

About 6 servings

325g jar lemon curd
500g carton Greek yogurt, chilled
4 meringue nests or about 60g/2¼ oz meringues

1. Tip the lemon curd into a jug and, with a whisk, stir in the yogurt.
2. Cover and chill for about 30 minutes.
3. Tip the mixture into the ice cream machine and freeze according to instructions.
4. Meanwhile, crush the meringues.
5. Transfer to a suitable container and gently stir in the crushed meringue.
6. Freeze until required.

Raspberry Ice

Any summer berry will work well in this yogurt ice – try blackberries, blueberries or blackcurrants.

About 6 servings

225g/8 oz fresh raspberries, thawed if frozen
100g/3½ oz golden caster sugar
500g carton plain Greek yogurt, chilled

1. Tip the raspberries and sugar into a food processor or blender and purée until smooth.
2. Pass the mixture through a non-metallic sieve to remove the seeds.
3. With a whisk, stir the yogurt into the fruit purée.
4. Cover and chill for about 30 minutes.
5. Tip the mixture into the ice cream machine and freeze according to instructions.
6. Transfer to a suitable container and freeze until required.

Peaches and Dream

When I am in Greece, my breakfast consists of a ripe, sun-warm peach served with thick Greek yogurt and drizzled with thyme honey. Canned peaches don't have the same allure but they make a lovely yogurt ice. The addition of white chocolate was my daughter's suggestion.

About 6 servings

410g can peaches in syrup
500g carton Greek yogurt
2 tbsp clear honey
100g/3½ oz white chocolate

1. Tip the peaches and their syrup into a food processor or blender.
2. Add the yogurt and honey and purée until smooth.
3. Tip into a jug, cover and refrigerate for about 30 minutes or until well chilled.
4. Meanwhile, chop the chocolate finely.
5. Tip the mixture into the ice cream machine and freeze according to instructions.
6. Add the chocolate for the final minute or two of churning.
7. Transfer to a suitable container and freeze until required.

Orange-Flower and Honey Ice

This is perfect for serving with any dessert made with nuts or pastry or both. Of course it is delicious just as it is, perhaps sprinkled with a few chopped pistachios, walnuts or pecan nuts.

About 4–6 servings

500g carton Greek yogurt, chilled
5 tbsp clear honey
2 tbsp orange-flower water

1. Tip the yogurt into a large jug.
2. With a whisk, stir in the honey and orange-flower water.
3. Cover and refrigerate for about 30 minutes or until well chilled.
4. Tip the mixture into the ice cream machine and freeze according to instructions.
5. Transfer to a suitable container and freeze until required.

9

DAIRY-FREE ICES

The recipes in this section include just a small selection of ices that are made without dairy produce like milk, cream, custard and cheese. Instead, they make use of soya products such as milk, cream and tofu. I hope they will be an inspiration for those who, for one reason or another, want to cut down on their dairy consumption. Though I have not yet tried, I see little reason why other recipes in this book could not be made by replacing dairy products with soya ones. I look forward to testing them myself.

Strawberry Ice

Soft fruits, such as raspberries, blackberries, blueberries and stoned cherries work well in this mixture too.

About 4 servings

350g/12 oz ripe strawberries
300ml/½ pint soya milk, chilled
175g/6 oz silken tofu, chilled
½ tsp vanilla extract
About 3 tbsp golden caster sugar

1. Remove the leafy hulls from the strawberries.
2. Put the strawberries into a food processor or blender.
3. Add the soya milk, tofu, vanilla and sugar to taste.
4. Purée until smooth.
5. Cover and chill for about 30 minutes.
6. Pour the mixture into the ice cream machine and freeze according to instructions.
7. Transfer to a suitable container and freeze until required.

Peach, Honey and Almond Ice

This is a basic recipe for using canned fruits. Try pineapple and coconut or pear and walnut. Use a well-flavoured honey, such as orange blossom.

About 4 servings

410g can peach halves in fruit juice
250ml carton soya cream, chilled
175g/6 oz silken tofu, chilled
About 3 tbsp clear honey
4 tbsp toasted flaked almonds

1. Drain the peaches and put them into a food processor or blender.
2. Add the soya cream, tofu and honey to taste.
3. Purée until smooth.
4. Cover and chill for about 30 minutes.
5. Pour the mixture into the ice cream machine and freeze according to instructions.
6. Add the almonds during the final minute or two of churning.
7. Transfer to a suitable container and freeze until required.

Apricot Soya Ice

This is equally good made with cherry, rhubarb or peach compote. Serve it with crisp biscuits such as ratafias or amaretti.

About 6–8 servings

600g jar apricot compote
4 tbsp clear honey
Two 250ml cartons soya cream, chilled
2 tbsp apricot or almond liqueur (optional)

1. Tip the apricot compote into a large jug and add the honey. Stir in the remaining ingredients.
2. Cover and refrigerate for about 30 minutes or until well chilled.
3. Tip the mixture into the ice cream machine and freeze according to instructions.
4. Transfer to a suitable container and freeze until required.

Orange Meringue Crunch

The bitter taste of the oranges is offset by the sweetness of the meringue.

About 6 servings

450g jar orange marmalade
Two 250g cartons soya cream, chilled
4 meringue nests or about 60g/2¼ oz meringues

1. Tip the marmalade into a jug and, with a whisk, stir in the soya cream.
2. Cover and chill for about 30 minutes.
3. Tip the mixture into the ice cream machine and freeze according to instructions.
4. Meanwhile, crush the meringues.
5. Transfer to a suitable container and gently stir in the crushed meringue.
6. Freeze until required.

Apple and Mint Ice

This refreshing ice is also good with some chunks of chocolate or carob bar stirred in just before freezing in step 5.

About 4–6 servings

475g jar apple sauce
Two 250ml cartons soya cream, chilled
About 4 tbsp mint jelly
Golden caster sugar (optional)

1. Tip the apple sauce into a large jug and add the soya cream. Stir in the mint jelly.
2. Cover and refrigerate for about 30 minutes or until well chilled.
3. Stir well and taste, adding extra mint jelly or a little sugar if necessary.
4. Tip the mixture into the ice cream machine and freeze according to instructions.
5. Transfer to a suitable container and freeze until required.

10

SORBETS AND GRANITAS

A sorbet is a smooth and refreshing water ice that is usually (though not always) made with fruit and sugar syrup. Sometimes sorbets are boosted by the addition of alcohol. An ice cream machine will make beautifully light sorbets that are ideal for serving as a light dessert or between courses as a palate freshener. I like to serve them within a few hours of making them, while they are still fairly soft and slushy. However, sorbets that have been allowed to freeze hard need only a brief time to soften up – take them out of the freezer and put them into the refrigerator about 15 minutes before serving.

A granita is similar to a sorbet but it is not nearly so smooth – it consists of much larger, crunchy ice crystals. Though a granita is best made by hand (not in an ice cream machine), the recipes that follow compromise by starting the freezing and churning process in the ice cream machine before transferring the mixture to the freezer to finish it off. I have given one recipe (Tomato, Chilli and Vodka Granita on page 95) that includes full instructions for making it by hand – just in case, like me, you prefer this method.

Melon and Lime Sorbet

Use a ripe melon that tastes really good; the lime juice lifts the flavour nicely. The colour of the sorbet will be dictated by the colour of the melon flesh – choose Galia for green, Charentais for orange, and so on.

About 4–6 servings

1 large melon
150g/5½ oz caster sugar
2 small limes

1. Cut the melon in half and scoop out and discard the seeds. Scoop out the flesh and weigh – you will need about 450g/1 lb.
2. Tip the melon flesh into a food processor or blender, add the sugar and purée until smooth.
3. Halve the limes and squeeze their juice. Add the lime juice to the melon mixture and purée briefly.
4. Transfer to a jug, cover and refrigerate for about 30 minutes or until well chilled.
5. Tip the mixture into the ice cream machine and freeze according to instructions.
6. Transfer to a suitable container or into four moulds and freeze until required.

Tropical Fruit Sorbet

For a beautiful colour and the best flavour, make sure the fruit you choose is ripe and juicy. Serve the sorbet with a fresh fruit salad, made with the same fruits, and some crisp biscuits (preferably containing coconut). You could also make this recipe with just one type of fruit, such as mango or papaya.

About 4–6 servings

225g/8 oz chopped mixed fruit, such as mango, papaya and pineapple
150g/5½ oz caster sugar
1 tbsp lime juice

1. Tip the fruit into a food processor or blender. Add the sugar, lime juice and 200ml/7 fl oz water. Purée until smooth.
2. Transfer to a jug, cover and refrigerate for about 30 minutes or until well chilled.
3. Tip the mixture into the ice cream machine and freeze according to instructions.
4. Transfer to a suitable container and freeze until required.

Raspberry Sorbet

A personal favourite of mine! For a perfectly smooth result, it's important to sieve the seeds out of the raspberry purée.

About 6 servings

115g/4 oz granulated sugar
450g/1 lb fresh raspberries, thawed if frozen
1 lemon

1. Put the sugar into a saucepan and add 150ml/¼ pint water. Heat gently, stirring, until the sugar has dissolved. Increase the heat and boil rapidly for about 5 minutes until the mixture looks syrupy. Remove from the heat and leave to cool.
2. Meanwhile, put the raspberries into a food processor or blender and purée until smooth. Pass the mixture through a non-metallic sieve to remove the seeds.
3. Squeeze the juice from the lemon.
4. Tip the syrup into a large jug and stir in the raspberry purée, and lemon juice.
5. Cover and refrigerate for about 30 minutes or until well chilled.
6. Tip the mixture into the ice cream machine and freeze according to instructions.
7. Transfer to a suitable container and freeze until required.

Lemon Sorbet

This recipe contains raw egg white (*see note on page 25*)*. You could, of course, omit it, though I think its addition makes for a nicer result. If you can't get unwaxed lemons, be sure to give the fruit a good scrub before paring off the rind.*

About 6 servings

3 unwaxed lemons
225g/8 oz granulated sugar
2 egg whites

1. Thinly pare the rind from the lemons (taking care to leave the white pith behind) and squeeze their juice.
2. Put the sugar and lemon rind into a saucepan and add 425ml/¾ pint water. Heat gently, stirring, until the sugar has dissolved. Increase the heat and boil rapidly for about 5 minutes until the mixture looks syrupy. Remove from the heat and leave to cool.
3. Add the lemon juice to the syrup and strain through a non-metallic sieve into a jug.
4. Lightly beat the egg whites and stir them in.
5. Cover and refrigerate for about 30 minutes or until well chilled.
6. Tip the mixture into the ice cream machine and freeze according to instructions.
7. Transfer to a suitable container and freeze until required.

Grapefruit and Gin Sorbet

I use a chilled carton of squeezed grapefruit juice though you could, of course, use the freshly squeezed juice of whole grapefruits. It's also good made with orange juice.

About 6 servings

150g/5½ oz granulated sugar
500ml/18 fl oz grapefruit juice
4 tbsp gin

1. Put the sugar into a saucepan and add 300ml/½ pint water. Heat gently, stirring, until the sugar has dissolved. Increase the heat and boil rapidly for about 5 minutes until the mixture looks syrupy. Remove from the heat and leave to cool.
2. Stir the grapefruit juice into the syrup.
3. Cover and refrigerate for about 30 minutes or until well chilled.
4. Stir in the gin.
5. Tip the mixture into the ice cream machine and freeze according to instructions.
6. Transfer to a suitable container and freeze until required.

Passion Fruit Sorbet

Choose fruits that are dark and wrinkly – these are really ripe and will have the best flavour.

About 4–6 servings

1 tsp powdered gelatine
2 lemons
250g/9 oz granulated sugar
8 passion fruits

1. Measure 2 tbsp water into a small bowl or cup, sprinkle the gelatine over and leave to stand for 5 minutes. Squeeze the juice from the lemons.
2. Put the sugar into a saucepan and add 300ml/½ pint water. Heat gently, stirring, until the sugar has dissolved. Increase the heat and boil rapidly for about 5 minutes until the mixture looks syrupy.
3. Remove from the heat, add the lemon juice then stir in the gelatine until it has dissolved.
4. Halve the passion fruits and, with a small spoon, scoop out the seeds and pulp into the syrup. Leave to cool.
5. Cover and refrigerate for at least 30 minutes or until well chilled.
6. Pass the chilled syrup through a non-metallic sieve to remove the seeds.
7. Tip the mixture into the ice cream machine and freeze according to instructions.
8. Transfer to a suitable container and freeze until required.

Pineapple Sorbet

I have also made this successfully with drained canned pineapple in fruit juice. Try adding a couple of tablespoonfuls of rum too. Please note that this recipe contains raw egg white (see page 25).

About 6 servings

375g/12 oz fresh pineapple pieces
1 lemon
150g/5½ oz caster sugar
½ tsp vanilla extract
2 egg whites

1. Put the pineapple into a food processor or blender and purée until very finely chopped.
2. Squeeze the juice from the lemon and add to the pineapple. Either add the sugar, vanilla and egg whites to the processor/blender and purée again (if the capacity is large enough), or tip the pineapple into a large jug and stir in the ingredients (beating the egg whites lightly first).
3. Cover and refrigerate for at least 30 minutes or until well chilled.
4. Tip the mixture into the ice cream machine and freeze according to instructions.
5. Transfer to a suitable container and freeze until required.

Apple and Mint Sorbet

Use a good quality apple juice for best results. Serve decorated with fresh mint leaves.

About 4–6 servings

100g/3½ oz golden granulated sugar
5 large sprigs of mint
425ml/¾ pint apple juice

1. Put the sugar into a saucepan and add the mint sprigs and 300ml/½ pint water. Heat gently, stirring, until the sugar has dissolved. Increase the heat and boil rapidly for about 5 minutes until the mixture looks syrupy.
2. Remove from the heat and stir in the apple juice.
3. Cover and refrigerate for at least 30 minutes or until well chilled.
4. Strain the mixture to remove the mint.
5. Tip into the ice cream machine and freeze according to instructions.
6. Transfer to a suitable container and freeze until required.

Tea Sorbet

Use your favourite tea – I particularly like green tea or Earl Grey.

About 4–6 servings

1 small unwaxed lemon
175g/6 oz golden caster sugar
2 teabags

1. Thinly pare the rind from the lemon (taking care to leave the white pith behind).
2. Put the sugar in a saucepan with 600ml (1 pint) water and heat gently until the sugar has dissolved. (Alternatively, put them into a suitable bowl and microwave on High, stirring occasionally, until the sugar has dissolved.)
3. Add the lemon rind to the sugar mixture and boil for 5–10 minutes until slightly syrupy.
4. Pour 150ml (¼ pint) boiling water over the tea bags and leave to infuse for 5 minutes. Remove the tea bags (squeezing out the liquor) and discard. Add the tea liquor to the sugar solution and leave to cool.
5. Cover and refrigerate for 30 minutes or until well chilled.
6. Strain into the ice cream machine and freeze according to instructions.
7. Transfer to a container, cover and store in the freezer. It will probably need stirring after about the first 45 minutes of freezing.

Coffee Granita

I make this with espresso or strong filter coffee, which must be freshly made. Serve in small chilled coffee cups or glasses and top with a spoonful of whipped cream and a couple of chocolate-coated coffee beans. For Coffee Sorbet, simply leave the mixture in the ice cream machine for the full freezing process – the ice crystals will be small with a pale colour and smooth texture.

About 6–8 servings

600ml/1 pint strong coffee
115g/4 oz caster sugar
2 tbsp coffee liqueur

1. As soon as you have made the coffee, add the sugar and stir until dissolved.
2. Leave to cool and then stir in the liqueur.
3. Cover and refrigerate for about 30 minutes or until well chilled.
4. Tip the mixture into the ice cream machine and freeze according to instructions. As soon as ice crystals begin to form, transfer to a shallow container.
5. Freeze until a thick layer of large ice crystals has formed around the edges.
6. Using a fork, break up the ice into smaller pieces and stir them into the centre of the container.
7. Freeze again repeating steps 4 and 5 until the mixture resembles crunchy crushed ice.

Tomato, Chilli and Vodka Granita

This is based on a recipe devised with fellow food writer Norma Miller during a photography session for a popular brand of organic pasta sauces. The jar was used to measure the vodka and water. It tasted just delicious. You could also make it by using a plain Italian-style tomato sauce and add some finely chopped red chilli.

About 4 servings

250g jar good quality tomato sauce with chilli
vodka
2 handfuls of chopped celery leaves

1. Tip the jar of sauce into a shallow freezer container.
2. Half fill the jar with vodka and top up to the rim with cold water. Add the mixture to the sauce and stir in.
3. Stir in the celery leaves, reserving some for garnish. Mix until well combined.
4. Freeze for about 5 hours until solid, stirring the frozen areas from the edges to the centre of the container about every hour if possible.
5. About 30 minutes before serving, break up the mixture with a fork. Return the crunchy mixture to the freezer for 30 minutes.
6. Spoon into glasses and serve immediately, garnished with celery leaves.

Lemon and Lime Granita

Taste the mixture before you put it into the ice cream machine so you can adjust the sharpness of the fruit or the sweetness of the sugar to your taste.

About 6 servings

2 lemons
2 limes
150g/5½ oz golden caster sugar

1. Squeeze the juice from the lemons and limes into a large jug. Add the sugar and 300ml/½ pint water.
2. Cover and refrigerate for about 30 minutes or until the sugar has dissolved and the mixture is well chilled.
3. Tip the mixture into the ice cream machine and freeze according to instructions. As soon as ice crystals begin to form, transfer to a shallow container.
4. Freeze until a thick layer of large ice crystals has formed around the edges.
5. Using a fork, break up the ice into smaller pieces and stir them into the centre of the container.
6. Freeze again repeating steps 4 and 5 until the mixture resembles crunchy crushed ice.

11

FROSTY DESSERTS

Ice creams can be moulded into amazing creations to make wonderful and unusual desserts. Try some of the ideas on the following pages and you will see just what I mean. There are the old favourites, such as Banana Splits and Baked Alaska, together with more trendy suggestions, such as Ice Cream Pie and Ice Cream Sandwiches. No doubt you will come up with some exciting ideas of your own too.

Cassata

This simple dessert is a variation of the Italian Cassata Gelata, where a mould is lined with layers of ice cream.

You will need to make two types of ice cream – such as Coffee and Walnut Ice Cream (page 65) and Tutti Frutti Rice Ice (page 67). Freeze them until they are soft and firm but not solid. Spoon the Coffee and Walnut Ice Cream into a pudding bowl, spreading it over the base and sides and leaving the centre free. Then fill the centre with the Tutti Frutti Rice Ice and freeze until very firm. Turn it out on to a serving plate by dipping the basin briefly (about 15–30 seconds) into hot water to loosen it first. If the ice cream is really hard, leave it in the refrigerator for about 20 minutes to soften slightly before serving. Serve cut into wedges.

Peach Melba

A dessert created in the late nineteenth century by the French chef Escoffier for the Australian opera singer Dame Nellie Melba. It consists of vanilla ice cream topped with peaches and raspberry sauce. Serve it in sundae glasses.

Purée some fresh raspberries by whizzing them in a food processor or blender, pass through a non-metallic sieve to remove the seeds, then sweeten to taste with icing sugar. Put a scoop of Vanilla Ice Cream (page 28 or 29) into each glass and place a drained, canned peach half on top. Spoon some raspberry sauce over and serve immediately.

Banana Splits

This was a popular choice in cafés when I was a young girl. You need to be hungry to eat this!

For each person, halve a banana lengthways and place on an individual serving plate. On top, arrange three scoops of ice cream (flavours of your choice but traditionally vanilla, strawberry and chocolate) and top these with whipped cream, chopped nuts and a maraschino cherry. Finally, drizzle some Chocolate or Butterscotch Sauce (pages 109 and 107) over the lot.

Ice Cream Bombe

This is simply ice cream that has been frozen in a spherical mould such as a pudding bowl. Use a single flavour or layers of ice cream and/or sorbet. You could serve it with your favourite sauce.

Freeze the ice creams until they are soft and firm but not solid. Spoon, one layer at a time, into the mould then freeze it until firm. Turn the bombe out on to a serving plate by dipping the basin briefly (about 15–30 seconds) into hot water to loosen it first. If the ice cream is really hard, leave it in the refrigerator for about 20 minutes to soften slightly before serving. Serve cut into wedges.

Fruit Bombe

Freeze the ice cream until soft and firm but not solid. Spoon it into a pudding bowl, spreading it over the base and sides and leaving the centre free. Then fill the centre with lightly cooked fruit (try raspberries, blackberries, plums) or canned fruit (apricots, peaches and pears are good) – I like to lace the fruit with some alcohol, such as brandy, rum or liqueur. Top with more ice cream to make a lid, sealing the fruit inside. Freeze until firm. Turn the bombe out on to a serving plate by dipping the basin briefly (about 15–30 seconds) into hot water to loosen it first. If the ice cream is really hard, leave it in the refrigerator for about 20 minutes to soften slightly before serving. Serve cut into wedges.

Praline Bombe

Line the basin with ice cream as for Fruit Bombe, but fill the centre with a mixture of whipped cream and crushed Praline (page 116).

Baked Alaska

Everyone seems to remember their surprise and delight on first tasting this concoction.

You will need a sponge flan case or a single layer of sponge cake. Make a meringue topping by whisking 2 medium egg whites until stiff peaks form, then folding in 85g/3 oz caster sugar. On top of the sponge (which could be moistened with a little sherry first) place a mound of ice cream, leaving the edges of the cake free. Swirl meringue over the top, covering the ice cream completely right to the edges of the cake. Now bake it in a hot oven (230°C, 450°F or Gas 8) for a few minutes until the meringue just begins to turn golden brown. Serve immediately.

Pear and Chocolate Sundae

This dessert is often called Belle Hélène or Poire Hélène.

Into individual glasses, put a generous scoop of Vanilla Ice Cream (page 28 or 29) and top with a pear half (this could be fresh fruit poached in vanilla syrup or drained canned pears). Pour warm Chocolate Sauce (page 109) over and, if that's not enough, you add a little whipped cream too.

Knickerbocker Glory

The mother of ice cream sundaes, it was made popular in the 1960s.

Simply layer chopped set jelly, fruit (preferably canned) and ice cream in tall sundae glasses and top with whipped cream and glacé cherries.

Chocolate Nut Sundae

An all-time favourite with the children in my family.

Put a scoop of Vanilla Ice Cream (page 28 or 29) into a sundae glass and coat with warm Chocolate Sauce (page 109). Add a swirl of cream and sprinkle with chopped nuts such as walnuts.

Ice Slice

I like to freeze ice cream in shapes – to make serving neat and easy, particularly at a smart dinner. Choose flavours and colours that taste and look good together. Serve it with or without a sauce.

You will need to make two or three types of ice cream and freeze them until they are soft and firm but not solid. Spoon one type into the bottom of a rectangular loaf tin and freeze until firm. Repeat with one or two more layers. Turn the loaf out on to a serving plate by dipping the basin briefly (about 15–30 seconds) into hot water to loosen it first. If the ice cream is really hard, leave it in the refrigerator for about 20 minutes to soften slightly before serving. Serve cut into slices.

Amaretti Ice Slice

Freeze Amaretti Ice (page 45) in a loaf tin and, as soon as it has been turned out, press finely crushed amaretti biscuits on to the top and sides. Serve it sliced with The Simplest Apricot Sauce (page 106).

Banana and Chocolate Ice Cream Pie

This dessert can easily be adapted – try chopped ready-to-eat apricots in place of bananas with Amaretti Ice (page 45) and grated white chocolate on top.

Freeze the Chocolate Ice Cream (page 30) until soft and firm but not solid. Slice a couple of bananas, toss in lemon juice and arrange them in the base of a cooked sweet pastry case or a biscuit crust (crushed biscuits mixed with melted butter and spread over the base and sides of a flan tin). Spread the ice cream over the bananas and level the surface. Top with crumbled flake bars and freeze for about 1 hour before serving.

Ice Cream Pancakes

Make some pancakes and serve them hot topped with a scoop of ice cream, some fresh fruit, chopped nuts and your favourite sauce.

Ice Cream Cake, Ice Cream Roulade and Ice Cream Sandwiches

These three delightful suggestions are from my good friend, the food writer Caroline Young, who is always brimming with ideas and eager to share them.

To make the **cake**, you will need two layers of sponge cake. Make your chosen ice cream and freeze it in a tin that is the same shape and width as the cake. When it is really firm, turn it out of the tin (by dipping the basin briefly into hot water to loosen it first) and sandwich it between the cake layers. With a palette knife, spread more ice cream on top and pop the whole cake into the freezer until required. Caroline says, “If it’s a birthday cake, don’t forget to insert the candle holders before you freeze the cake.” To serve it, transfer the cake to the refrigerator for about 20 minutes to soften slightly.

Make your favourite sponge or meringue **roulade**, fill it with ice cream and freeze until required. Serve with fresh soft fruit and Berry Fruit Sauce (page 112).

Sandwich together your favourite large soft cookies (preferably home-made) with a thick layer of ice cream. Either eat immediately or freeze until you can’t resist them any longer.

12

SAUCES AND TOPPINGS FOR ICE CREAM

A sauce or topping can jazz up the plainest of ice creams.

Sauces in their simplest form include warmed honey, maple syrup or, my favourite, malt extract. Or try melting jams, jellies or chocolate bars and just drizzle them over your favourite ice cream.

For a crunchy topping try chopped nuts, crushed biscuits such as amaretti, chopped chocolate, crumbled flake bars or whole chocolate buttons.

With only slightly more effort you could make the recipes on the following pages too. They are all yummy!

Orange and Lemon Sauce

This is also good made with apple juice instead of orange juice and served with the Ginger Ice Cream on page 66.

About 8 servings

1 large unwaxed lemon
3 tbsp caster sugar
2 tbsp cornflour
450ml/16 fl oz orange juice

1. Finely grate the rind from the lemon and squeeze out its juice.
2. Put the sugar and cornflour into a small saucepan and mix well. (Alternatively, put them into a microwaveable bowl.)
3. Whisk in the orange juice.
4. Heat, stirring, until the mixture comes to the boil and is thickened and smooth. (Or microwave on High for about 3 minutes, stirring frequently, until the mlxture comes to the boil and is thickened and smooth.)
5. Remove from the heat and stir in the lemon rind and juice.
6. Serve hot or warm.

The Simplest Apricot Sauce

You cannot get much quicker or simpler than these two versions – one hot and one chilled.

About 4 servings

About 8 tbsp apricot jam
About 1½ tbsp lemon juice

1. Put the jam and lemon juice into a small pan and heat gently, stirring, until bubbling hot. (Alternatively, put them into a suitable small bowl, microwave on Medium for 1½–2 minutes until hot and stir well.)
2. Serve immediately.

400g can apricot halves in fruit juice
caster sugar

1. Drain the apricots and put them into a food processor or blender. Purée until smooth.
2. Add caster sugar to taste.
3. Chill until required.

Butterscotch Sauce

It's particularly good with ice creams that contain bananas or chocolate. If you like a bit of crunch then stir in about 25g/1 oz broken walnuts before serving. You may prefer to serve it with an ice cream that has its own crunch – like Chunky Pecan and Maple Ice Cream on page 48.

About 6 servings

55g/2 oz butter
55g/2 oz muscovado sugar
175g/6 oz golden syrup
2 tsp lemon juice
150ml/¼ pt double cream

1. Put the butter, sugar and syrup into a small pan. (Alternatively, put them into a microwaveable bowl.)
2. Heat gently, stirring occasionally, until the butter has melted. Stir until well blended. (Or microwave on High for about 2 minutes, stirring once or twice, until the butter has melted. Stir until well blended.)
3. Stir in the lemon juice and cream and heat gently until bubbling. (Or stir in the lemon juice and cream and cook on High for ½–1 minute or until just bubbling.)
4. Serve warm.

Rum Syrup Sauce

Serve in particular with Vanilla and Chocolate Chip Ice Cream (page 43), Mango Ice Cream (page 37) or Coconut Ice (page 49).

About 6 servings

175g/6 oz golden syrup
75g/2¾ oz light muscovado sugar
50g/1¾ oz butter
5 tbsp single cream
2 tbsp lemon juice
3 tbsp dark rum

1. Put the syrup into a small saucepan and add the sugar and butter. (Alternatively, put them into a microwave-able bowl.)
2. Heat gently, stirring occasionally, until the butter has melted and the sugar has dissolved. (Or microwave on High for about 2 minutes, stirring once, until the butter has melted and the sugar has dissolved.)
3. Stir in the cream and then the lemon juice and rum.
4. Serve warm.

Chocolate Sauce

For a good flavour, use a plain chocolate with about 50 per cent cocoa solids. You could give it a boost by stirring in one or two tablespoonfuls of orange liqueur just before serving.

About 6 servings

175g/6 oz plain chocolate
3 tbsp golden syrup
1 tbsp fresh lemon or orange juice
small piece of butter

1. Break the chocolate into a small pan and add the syrup, juice, butter and 2 tbsp water. (Alternatively, put them into a microwaveable bowl.)
2. Heat gently, stirring occasionally, until the chocolate has melted and is smooth and glossy. (Or microwave on Medium for 2–3 minutes, stirring frequently, until the chocolate has melted and is smooth and glossy.)
3. Serve hot or warm.

Melba Sauce

If you like a really smooth sauce, sieve out the seeds before serving.

About 4–6 servings

6 tbsp redcurrant jelly
6 tbsp raspberry jam
3 tbsp lemon juice

1. Put the jelly, jam and lemon juice into a small saucepan. (Alternatively, put them into a microwaveable bowl.)
2. Heat gently, stirring, until melted and bubbling. (Or microwave on High for 2–3 minutes, whisking frequently, until melted and bubbling.)
3. Serve hot or warm.

Gingery Fudge Sauce

It's simply lovely with Rhubarb and Custard Ice (page 46), Pear and Amaretti Ice (page 53) or Brown Bread Ice Cream (page 63).

About 8 servings

170g can evaporated milk
150g/5½ oz light muscovado sugar
50g/1¾ oz butter
1½ tsp ground ginger

1. Pour the evaporated milk into a small pan and add the sugar, butter and ginger. (Alternatively, put them into a microwaveable bowl.)
2. Heat, gently, stirring occasionally, until the sugar has dissolved. Continue heating until the sauce comes to the boil and bubble gently for a few minutes. (Or microwave on High for 2–3 minutes, stirring frequently, until the sugar has dissolved and the sauce is bubbling.)
3. Serve warm or at room temperature.

Maple Sauce

Delicious with Almond and Chocolate Raisin Ice Cream (page 50), Coffee and Walnut Ice Cream (page 65) or Toasted Apple and Cinnamon Ice (page 56).

About 6 servings

50g/1¾ oz butter
25g/1 oz golden caster sugar
4 tbsp maple syrup
150ml/¼ pt double cream

1. Put the butter, sugar, syrup and cream into a small saucepan. (Alternatively, put them into a microwaveable bowl.)
2. Heat gently, stirring frequently, until the sugar has dissolved and the mixture comes to the boil. Bubble gently for a minute or two. (Or microwave on High for about 2 minutes, stirring frequently, until the sugar has dissolved and the mixture is bubbling.)
3. Serve warm.

Berry Fruit Sauce

For this fresh-tasting sauce, use one type of berry (raspberries are excellent) or a mixture – such as raspberries, blackberries, strawberries, blackcurrants, redcurrants and blueberries in any combination.

About 6 servings

250g/9 oz summer berries, thawed if frozen
2 tsp lemon juice
icing sugar
2 tbsp fruit liqueur, such as orange, raspberry (framboise) or blackcurrant (cassis)

1. Tip the fruit into a food processor or liquidiser and add the lemon juice and 2 tbsp sugar.
2. Purée until smooth.
3. Adjust the sweetness, adding sugar to taste.
4. Pass the sauce through a fine nylon sieve to remove the seeds.
5. Stir in the liqueur.
6. Serve at room temperature or gently warmed through.

Rum and Raisin Sauce

Good on vanilla or chocolate ice cream.

About 6 servings

50g/1¾ oz butter
50g/1¾ oz light muscovado sugar
284ml carton double cream
4 tbsp dark rum
50g/1¾ oz raisins

1. Put the butter and sugar into a small saucepan. (Alternatively, put them into a microwaveable bowl.)
2. Heat gently, stirring, until the sugar has dissolved. (Or microwave on High for ½-1 minute, stirring once, until the butter has melted and the sugar has dissolved.)
3. Add the cream and rum and bubble gently for 2–3 minutes. (Or microwave on High for about 2 minutes, stirring once, until bubbling.)
4. Remove from the heat, stir in the raisins and leave to stand for 5 minutes.
5. Serve warm.

Coffee Caramel Sauce

Good with Almond and Chocolate Raisin Ice Cream (page 50), Chocolate Honeycomb Ice Cream (page 55) or any vanilla ice cream.

About 4 servings

Two 50g bars chocolate caramel
200ml/7 fl oz milk
2 tsp good quality instant coffee granules

1. Break the chocolate bars into squares and put into a small pan with the milk and coffee. (Alternatively, put them into a microwaveable bowl.)
2. Heat gently, stirring, until the caramel and coffee have dissolved and the sauce is smooth. (Or microwave on High for about 1 minute, stirring occasionally, until the caramel and coffee have dissolved and the sauce is smooth.)
3. Serve immediately.

Raspberry and Orange-Flower Sauce

Particularly delightful served with Strawberry Pavlova Ripple (page 35) or Strawberries and Clotted Cream (page 39).

About 4–6 servings

250g/9 oz fresh raspberries, thawed if frozen
25g/1 oz caster sugar
1 tbsp orange-flower water

1. Put the raspberries into a food processor or blender and purée until smooth.
2. Pass the raspberry purée through a non-metallic sieve to remove the seeds.
3. Stir in the sugar and flower water.
4. Chill until required.

Granola Topping

Granola is just like toasted muesli. It can turn the simplest (and plainest) ice cream into something really memorable. It's worth making plenty because the mixture keeps well in an airtight container. Granola is also great served for breakfast (with milk or fruit juice) or as a snack nibble at any time of the day.

At least 10 servings

100g/3½ oz almonds, hazelnuts or brazils
250g/9 oz rolled oats
75g/2¾ oz sunflower seeds
75g/2¾ oz pumpkin seeds
50g/1¾ oz sesame seeds
50g/1¾ oz coconut shavings
4 tbsp safflower or sunflower oil
4 tbsp clear honey
1 tsp vanilla extract
50g/1¾ oz raisins

1. Preheat the oven to 150°C, 300°F or Gas 2.
2. Put the nuts into a food processor or blender and pulse on medium-low speed until roughly chopped.
3. Tip the chopped nuts into a large bowl and stir in the oats, seeds and coconut.
4. Whisk together the oil, honey and vanilla, and add to the bowl, stirring until the contents are well coated.
5. Spread the mixture in an even layer on a baking tray.
6. Put into the hot oven and bake for about 45 minutes, stirring frequently, until rich golden brown and quite dry.
7. Leave to cool (it will crisp up), stirring occasionally, then mix in the raisins.

Praline

Crush these caramelised almonds and scatter the mixture on top of your favourite ices. It keeps beautifully in a screw-top jar.

About 10 servings or more

Oil
100g/3½ oz whole almonds with skins
100g/3½ oz golden granulated sugar

1. Oil a baking sheet and set it on a heatproof surface.
2. Put the almonds and sugar into a small heavy-based saucepan. Put over a medium heat and stir until the sugar liquefies and then caramelises, so that the mixture is golden brown and the nuts are glazed. (Take care – it gets very hot!)
3. Quickly pour the mixture on to the oiled baking sheet and leave until completely cool and hard.
4. Break into pieces and crush finely (either with a rolling pin or by pulsing the mixture in a food processor).

13

SHAKES, SLUSHES AND CHILLY DRINKS

When my daughter was little, she insisted that when she grew up she would work in a shop that sold those popular brightly coloured slush drinks. Now she is adult, she has forsaken her childhood dream and replaced it with a blender in which she makes wonderful shakes and smoothies. I expect her next step to be the purchase of an ice cream machine – or maybe she is waiting for me to present her with one. After all, what can be more refreshing on an evening with friends, or on a warm summer's day, than a chilled drink made in the ice cream machine with the freshest ingredients? Would she not be the envy of all her friends?

I hope the ideas in this section will stimulate you to try even more exciting concoctions. Remember: once the drinks are made, don't be tempted to store them – they are best served as soon as they become iced and slushy. Be as elegant as you like and serve them in stunning, tall glasses with trendy, wide straws and a long-handled spoon to scoop up the last dregs of ice. Keep cool!

Iced Mango and Banana Shake

Serve in chilled tall glasses and decorate with thin slices of fresh orange.

About 4 servings

1 large ripe mango
1 large ripe banana
150ml/¼ pt orange juice
150ml/¼ pt milk
1 tbsp clear honey

1. With a sharp knife, cut the mango and remove its stone. Remove the flesh from the skin and put it into a food processor or blender.
2. Peel and break up the banana and add it to the mango with the orange juice, milk and honey.
3. Purée until smooth.
4. Pour the mixture into the ice cream machine and freeze according to instructions until icy cold.
5. Serve immediately.

Fruit Yogurt Slush

Use your favourite fruit-flavoured yogurt and serve with colourful, wide drinking straws.

About 4 servings

300ml/½ pt milk, chilled
500g carton strawberry yogurt, chilled
1 tbsp lemon juice
2 ripe bananas

1. Put the milk, yogurt and lemon juice into a food processor or blender.
2. Peel and break up the bananas and add to the milk mixture.
3. Purée until smooth.
4. Pour the mixture into the ice cream machine and freeze according to instructions until slushy with ice.
5. Serve immediately.

Spiced Iced Latte

To serve, top each glass with a swirl of whipped cream and a sprinkling of grated chocolate or sifted chocolate powder.

About 3–4 servings

425ml/¾ pt milk
425ml/¾ pt freshly made strong black coffee
½ tsp ground mixed spice

1. With a whisk, stir the ingredients together.
2. Pour the mixture into the ice cream machine and freeze according to instructions until icy cold.
3. Serve immediately.

Tropical Smoothie Slush

Sometimes, I add the pulp and seeds of a passion fruit to this mixture too. Be sure to serve it with long-handled spoons for easy scooping from the glass.

About 4 servings

1 small ripe pineapple
1 ripe mango
1 ripe banana
1 tbsp lime juice
About 300ml/½ pint orange juice

1. With a sharp knife, peel the pineapple, cut lengthways into quarters and remove the core. Cut into chunks.
2. Cut the mango, remove its stone and scoop the flesh from the skin.
3. Peel and break up the banana.
4. Put 225g/8 oz pineapple into a food processor or blender. Add the mango, banana, lime juice and orange juice.
5. Purée until smooth and thick.
6. Pour the mixture into the ice cream machine and freeze according to instructions until slushy.
7. Put the remaining pineapple chunks into chilled glasses and pour the slush over the top. Serve immediately.

Apricot Shake Cooler

Serve this summery drink in chilled glasses with wide straws. Adjust the sweetness with honey to suit your own taste. Make Peach Cooler by replacing the apricots with two large ripe peaches.

About 3–4 servings

6 ripe apricots
1 ripe banana
About 2 tbsp clear honey
600ml/1 pint milk

1. With a sharp knife, halve the apricots and remove their stones. Remove the flesh from the skin (not essential) and cut into chunks.
2. Peel and break up the banana.
3. Put all the ingredients into a food processor or blender and purée until smooth.
4. Pour the mixture into the ice cream machine and freeze according to instructions until icy cold.
5. Serve immediately.

Mango Lassi

This refreshing yogurt drink is delicious, particularly at the end of a spicy meal. The heat in your mouth will dissipate instantly! Serve it in small glasses.

About 3–4 servings

3 ripe mangoes
150g carton natural yogurt
3 tbsp lime juice
2 tbsp clear honey

1. With a sharp knife, cut the mangoes and remove their stones. Scoop the flesh from the skin and put into a food processor or blender.
2. Add the remaining ingredients to the mango and purée until smooth.
3. Pour the mixture into the ice cream machine and freeze according to instructions until icy cold.
4. Serve immediately.

Iced Raspberry Soya

Try using other soft fruits, such as strawberries, blackberries, blueberries or stoned cherries too.

About 4 servings

350g/12 oz ripe raspberries
300ml/½ pint soya milk
175g/6 oz silken tofu
2 tbsp clear honey
½ tsp vanilla extract

1. Put the raspberries into a food processor or blender.
2. Add the remaining ingredients.
3. Purée until smooth.
4. Pour the mixture into the ice cream machine and freeze according to instructions until icy cold and slightly slushy.
5. Serve immediately.

Five-Fruit Smoothie

This is a deliciously fresh pick-me-up on a warm summer day.

About 4 servings

3 bananas
6 ripe strawberries, leafy hulls removed
Small handful of fresh blueberries
300ml/½ pint cranberry juice
150ml/¼ pint orange juice

1. Peel the bananas and break them into a food processor or blender.
2. Add the remaining ingredients.
3. Purée until smooth.
4. Pour the mixture into the ice cream machine and freeze according to instructions until slushy.
5. Serve immediately.

Chocolate, Banana and Hazelnut Slush

To make this a dairy-free drink, use soya milk and chocolate syrup.

About 4 servings

2 bananas
600ml/1 pint milk
4 generous tbsp chocolate and hazelnut spread

1. Peel the bananas and break them into a food processor or blender.
2. Add the remaining ingredients.
3. Purée until smooth.
4. Pour the mixture into the ice cream machine and freeze according to instructions until slushy.
5. Serve immediately.

Iced Vodka Tomato Cocktail

Serve this in chilled glasses with a small stick of celery in each for stirring (and eating).

About 4 servings

200ml/7 fl oz vodka
400ml/14 fl oz tomato juice
2 tsp Worcestershire sauce
1 tbsp lemon juice
Few drops of hot chilli sauce

1. With a whisk, stir together the vodka, tomato juice, Worcestershire sauce, lemon juice and 200ml/7 fl oz water. Add chilli sauce to taste.
2. Pour the mixture into the ice cream machine and freeze according to instructions until icy cold.
3. Serve immediately.

Cranberry, Grapefruit and Rum Cooler

Serve in highball glasses, each decorated with a slice of lemon.

About 4 servings

300ml/½ pint cranberry juice
300ml/½ pint grapefruit juice
200ml/7 fl oz white rum

1. Combine the ingredients.
2. Pour the mixture into the ice cream machine and freeze according to instructions until icy cold and slightly slushy.
3. Serve immediately.

Gin and Elderflower Chill

This is one of those drinks that can be changed to suit whatever you have handy – blackcurrant cordial with rum and lime, cranberry cordial with vodka and orange, ginger cordial with whisky and lemon.

About 4 servings

150ml/¼ pint elderflower cordial
125ml/4 fl oz gin
1 lime

1. Mix the cordial with 600ml/1 pint water. Add the gin.
2. Halve the lime. Squeeze the juice of one half into the elderflower mixture.
3. Pour the mixture into the ice cream machine and freeze according to instructions until icy cold and slightly slushy.
4. Meanwhile, thinly slice the remaining lime half.
5. Serve immediately, decorated with lime slices.

INDEX